HARRY GORDON

'The Laird of Inversnecky'

Iain Watson

Project Co-ordinator and Editor: Jim Pratt
ISBN 0 946 920 09 5

City of Aberdeen   Arts and Recreation Division

F 2/GOR.
515292

Printed by BPCC-AUP Aberdeen Ltd.

CONTENTS

ACKNOWLEDGEMENTS

The author is most grateful to the following for their help: Bunty McLeod (Gordon), J. C. Parkinson, the late Howard Lockhart and Clement Ashby for providing him with original material and sharing personal reminiscences. Winifred Hyslop for access to manuscripts by A. F. Hyslop; Alistair Macdonald, Edwin Webster, Alan Cooper and Michael Thomson for their cheerful assistance; the staff of the Local Studies Section, Aberdeen City Library, Edinburgh Public Library and the Mitchell Library for their co-operation.

The Editor would like to acknowledge the assistance given to him by Mr. Archie Foley, Mr. Gordon Irving, Janet McBain and Anne Docherty of the Scottish Film Archive; Elizabeth Watson, Scottish Theatre Archive, Glasgow. He would also like to thank Mr. Robbie Shepherd and Mr. Ken Mutch of BBC Radio in Aberdeen for their support and interest.

Thanks also are extended to the many individuals who have taken the trouble to contact the Editor during the preparation of this biography.

1.   OVERTURE

Harry Gordon was described by Fenton Wyness in his history of Aberdeen - 'City by the Grey North Sea' - as "possibly the only real attraction Aberdeen beach has ever had", and it was at the Beach Pavilion where Harry Gordon, a native of the city, with his summer seasons of 'Harry Gordon and his Entertainers' in the 1920's and 1930's won for himself a special niche in the hearts of all Aberdonians. To many Harry was never better than in the easy intimate atmosphere of those successive Pavilions overlooking the sea. Inversnecky was born there - the fictitious village which incorporated all the facets of an ideal community in the North-East of Scotland, highly conscious of its individual identity. Harry Gordon's off-taking Inversnecky portraits were about universal phenomena but they had those shrewd local touches which Aberdonians delightedly recognised as peculiarly their own: portrayals of all the characters and institutions of the village were received with acclaim and affection.

Harry Gordon's reputation was however much more wide-spread. By the early 30's he had become an established pantomime star in Glasgow and Edinburgh, and modifying his Aberdeen patois, he contrived to be completely understood, without in any way sacrificing the verbal aplomb which was such an essential part of his style.

It was in Glasgow that he created the series of classic pantomime dame studies, which won him such praise and by which he is principally remembered in that city. In the South of Scotland he became the star of 'Half-Past Eight', and it was in this show that he made his only return visits with nostalgia and sometimes trepidation to Aberdeen after the Second World War. In England Harry Gordon's accent and his quick-fire patter made rather less impression, but he was immensely popular amongst exiled Scotsmen and made several successful tours of the North American continent.

Harry Gordon enjoys a reputation among the great figures of the Scottish variety theatre in the company of Sir Harry Lauder, Will Fyffe and Dave Willis, and while it is wrong to pretend he had a universal appeal, it would also be unfair to suggest that he was an entertainer who relied solely on parochial humour.

Nevertheless, despite his successes elsewhere, the Beach Pavilion, Aberdeen perhaps remains at the core of his career - as comedian and entrepreneur. No-one can fail to marvel at the magnetism of the man who could draw crowds to the windswept shoreline of Aberdeen beach, which the authorities to this day attempt to sell as a feature to prospective visitors.

It was all summed up in 'The Auldest Aiberdonion':

> "I can min' fin Bruce - the great King Robert - cam' by here,
> The Council held a banquet, aye the rates went up that year,
> They thankit Bruce for keepin' a' the English oot o' reach,
> Ye see, it hidna struck us then to advertise the beach."

2.   CURTAIN-UP

Harry Gordon was born on the 11th July,1893 at 7 Powis Place, Aberdeen. His full name was Alexander Ross Gordon but by an easy transposition the initials A. R. were reversed becoming R. A. and so "Harry". He was the eldest of a family of five sons and a daughter. His father, David Smith Gordon was a journeyman plumber who had worked on the building of His Majesty's Theatre, Aberdeen. Indeed Harry Gordon later used to joke that the Gordon family were built into the foundations of the theatre. He was brought up in a tenement in Urquhart Road, Aberdeen. In the same way that Sir Harry Lauder used to cause much laughter with his "I have just come from Strath Haven", using an exaggeratedly refined pronunciation of Strathaven which is usually pronounced "Straiven", Harry Gordon would in the 'Half-Past Eight' shows in Aberdeen occasionally introduce a reference to Urquhart Road. He would get one of the artists, often Clem Ashby, who had an English accent, to ask him the way to "Ur - queue - hart Road". After some misunderstandings Harry would roll out Urquhart Road in his strongest North East accent, an invariably successful ploy with his Aberdeen audience.

Harry Gordon was educated at King Street School and subsequently the Central School in Little Belmont Street, Aberdeen. He early demonstrated the strong influence that the theatre was to have on him - although in a somewhat surprising way. The play 'The Grip of Iron' was being presented at Her Majesty's Theatre, Guild Street, Aberdeen - later to become the Tivoli. The principal character in the play used a method of strangulation to kill off his victims. This set Harry's youthful imagination on fire and for weeks and months afterwards he practised this grip of iron. His victims were usually boys of his own age and size. Occasionally however, he sought older and bigger game, and one such exploit had rather painful consequences. One of his mother's acquaintances was a lady who on visits usually overstayed her welcome. It happened that she arrived one day when his mother was not prepared for callers and did not want them. "What a bother" - he heard her say - "I wonder how I am going to get rid of her?" An opportunity had presented itself for Harry and at a favourable moment, he climbed on to the visitor's knee. "Have you ever had a grip of iron?" he asked as he seized the astonished lady by the throat and compressed it in the approved style of his hero. This little bit of realistic acting aroused the anger of his mother who adopted her usual method of showing her displeasure. The recollecting of that chastisement suggested to young Harry that in future his acting activities should take a rather more verbal form.

Harry began to do impromptu character studies. He studied the distinctive features and foibles of his mother's lady visitors and when they had left he would copy the way they talked and acted. He was extremely observant and learned all the Aberdeen sayings and mannerisms. The props and clothes for these characters were readily to hand, for in the lobby of their house was a press (cupboard) filled with all sorts of clothing. This he claimed as his wardrobe and dressing room and he gave the members of his family much amusement by his make up and performances in character. Soon he was giving performances to his friends on the back green of his house.

Harry's traditional instincts revolted at the idea of giving these little shows free of charge. A jam tart, or a biscuit or some sweets were charged for admission.

Harry Gordon's first experience on a real stage came some time later. He was a Sunday School pupil at Gilcomston Parish Church, Summer Street, Aberdeen. This later became Gilcomston St. Colm's and later still the Denburn Church. At that time children's cantatas enjoyed considerable popularity and as a member of the Sunday School choir, he took part in many of these. Harry played the part of the Emperor What-for-Why in the cantata 'Princess Chrysanthemum' under the baton of John Hutcheson. The choice of Harry was apparently born of hope rather than any evidence of amazing talent, for in spite of the patience of the conductor, who took him through his songs at every opportunity, the night of the performance found him floundering so hopelessly that whenever he was due to sing, the performance had to be held up while the pianist thumped out the tune on the piano. However Harry was discovering that he had a natural aptitude for making people laugh and could put over a song successfully. One of the first comic songs he sang was "I'm the saftest o' the family". Seated up in the gallery of the Palace Theatre, Bridge Place, Aberdeen he had heard Harry Lauder sing the song and in his youthful imagination thought he could sing it as well as Lauder - his mother thought he could sing it better. In Harry Gordon's own words recalling this much later "I was gauin' wi' rowies and as I went roon' my roon' I practised the Lauder lilt" - and having perfected the song Harry performed it at a kirk soiree at Gilcomston Church.

Harry Gordon spent a good part of his school holidays in Torry with his uncle, Alec Ross, a trawler skipper. Occasionally he was allowed to go to sea along with another small boy and they had free access to the clothing of the crew. By way of relieving the tedium of the trip, they were frequently induced to dress up in sou'westers and reefers and give imitations of certain Aberdeen characters.

All this began to introduce into his mind, and to grow there, the idea of following the stage as a career. Eventually this grew to become his sole aim and object and as a beginning he found a footing on the concert platform in Aberdeen and district.

4

Harry's parents could not afford for him not to have a full time job, although they realised what his true ambition was. So Harry started work in the office of George Mollison & Sons, grain importers, as an office boy, becoming in time a junior clerk. His concert engagements gradually became more numerous, some more successful than others. He conceived a double act with another youth from Mollison's office named Mitchell. They were both extremely keen and rehearsed until they had, as they thought, a really professional act.

Under the high sounding name - 'The Two Savoys', their first engagement was at the Music Hall in Peterhead and it was two very anxious comedians who set out from Aberdeen. Their trepidation was fully justified when the Peterhead audience showed exactly what they thought of the performance: they tolerated them for about five minutes!

However, it all added to Harry Gordon's experience and with growing skill and greater success his concert engagements became more frequent. He was, however, still a junior clerk and was having to ask for leave of absence so often to go to concerts that, as a matter of office discipline, he was finally told that he would have to choose between his work and concert engagements. It had become impossible to reconcile the two as Gordon later recalled - "Asked to choose between the devil of working in a produce merchant's business and the deep blue sea of going on the stage, I at once dived out the door and into the deep sea. I canna swim ye ken - but that sounds nae bad - eh?". So it was that before his 15th birthday Harry Gordon decided on the concert platform and in later years he used to marvel at how he tilted at fate, most of the important decisions of his life having been taken when he was little more than a boy.

In 1908 Harry won a talent competition at the Aberdeen Beach Pavilion, the theatre which was later to play such an important part in his career. Then the following year he made his first business venture in association with Sandy Muchalls and the pianist Inkster Bannerman. The summer of 1909 was a slack period for concert engagements and the three of them conceived the idea of starting a pierrot troupe at the Deeside village of Banchory. They enlisted the services of Willie Smith, the Aberdeen baritone, the soprano Kate Morgan and the soubrette and dancer Jessie Dudgeon. The same age as Harry, Jessie Dudgeon had already had several dancing successes. In 1900 she had won the Scottish championship at the old theatre in Arbroath, then under the management of Dod Melvin, father of G. S. Melvin, the comedian who became famous for his grotesque characterisations. Jessie Dudgeon had also competed successfully at most of the Highland gatherings and had the distinction of winning the first prize three years running at the Braemar Gathering. Harry and

Jessie practised a number of double turns for the little pierrot show at Banchory, often slipping away from the rest of the company to be alone together. This was the beginning of their romance.

The Banchory performances were given entirely in the open air and the company's income was derived partly from the sale of very limited seating accommodation but mainly from collections among the audience. They did not make a fortune but they did make many good friends.

One day the troupe had an unexpected windfall. They thought it would be a good advertisement if they gave a performance to the patients at Glen o' Dee Sanitorium at Banchory. The medical superintendent stipulated that the performance should not last longer than about three quarters of an hour. The patients who came to hear them numbered about twenty and when at the close of the performance, the doctor suggested they make their usual collection, the troupe had hopes of an unexpected gain of a pound or so for the patients were all quite wealthy people. In fact the collection brought in over £6. Later on in the season, they offered to give another performance, but this time the doctor was adamant: "No, no" he said, "not any more. We cannot be too hard on the patients".

The winter following Harry's Banchory venture, he appeared with Jessie Dudgeon (her stage name was Jose Goray) as a double act mainly in the North-East of Scotland and they were greatly encouraged by the warm reception they received wherever they went.

It was when playing the Palace, Peterhead, where Harry Gordon worked hard to erase the memory of his previous engagement in the town, that he and Jessie Dudgeon, both aged 17, went away for the day to Aberdeen and were quietly married.

One of their touring engagements was in the Buchan village of Auchnagatt, where one of the company was a conjuror who rejoiced in the name of Mystic Vere. On another occasion Harry was booked to play two concerts at Fraserburgh, one in the Good Templar Hall, the other the following night in the Dalrymple Hall. Unfortunately this was at a time of terrific storms with road and train services at a standstill. The only way Harry could manage to get to Fraserburgh was on a tug boat which was carrying the mails to the beleagured town. It was a nightmare journey, but Harry fulfilled the engagement. Very flattering reference was made to Harry's courage, pluck and determination, and even if in his racked and weakened state he could not give of his best, the audiences were very sympathetic.

6

These local concerts were Harry's training ground and from there he graduated to the theatre proper; making his first appearance on the variety stage in 1910. This was at the old Empire in George Street, Aberdeen, a building which subsequently became offices for the Northern Friendly Society. The Empire was then run by James Montague (familiarly known as Monty) and Robert Calder, a pioneer of the cinematograph in Aberdeen and the North.

Harry Gordon owed much to both of these men not only for their help and advice but also in the more practical aspect of providing work. Following the engagement at the Empire, Robert Calder booked Harry Gordon for a tour of Orkney and Shetland with his travelling cinema. A highlight of that enterprise was a film showing scenes of the funeral of King Edward VII and it was part of Harry's duties to stand at the side of the screen and with a long pointer, indicate the various Royal personages who took part in the funeral procession.

Harry continued his association with Monty appearing with his troupe of pierrots at the Bannermill Gardens - which were situated at the foot of Constitution Street, Aberdeen. Nearby factories frequently used to generate an unpleasant smell, and the performers would have difficulty knowing whether it was the smell or the songs which caused the audience to melt away long before the collection bag was due.

He spent two happy seasons with Monty's Pierrots at Stonehaven and continued to appear in other seaside shows. In the summer of 1915 he was a member of Fred Collin's pierrot troupe at Burntisland in Fife at a salary of £3.00 a week. Sam Thomson, a Glasgow comedian of the old school, was principal comedian while Jack Holden who was later to be associated professionally so closely with Harry Gordon, was also a member of the company. Harry learned a great deal from Fred Collins, who was an extremely capable showman. His fertile brain evolved stunts designed to keep the pierrots in the forefront of the minds of the people of Burntisland and to ensure that new visitors were soon made aware of the troupe's existence. This search for novelty was a lesson Harry was to bear very much in mind when running his own summer seasons at the Aberdeen Beach Pavilion.

Amongst Harry's other engagements prior to his enlisting in 1915, were tours which came only as a result of his lengthy training in the halls of the North. He was introduced to Harry Milne, the variety agent and manager of Hengler's Circus in Glasgow. Harry Gordon and his wife were imediately booked for their first tour of the South of Scotland playing such towns as Broxburn, Larbert and Grangemouth. It was hard work. Harry and his wife had to do a single turn each as well as their double act. This meant that if there were two shows a night he had first to appear in comedy make-up, then black-up for their double turn, wash off the colour and go through the same procedure for the second house.

In 1915 Harry Gordon attested under the 'Derby' scheme and the story of his wartime activities is told in a later chapter. The war period may be said to mark a definite phase in the development of Gordon's music-hall career. Prior to 1915 he had been learning the ropes. Now he was able to apply his knowledge and skill to quickly further his chosen profession.

Immediately on demobilisation, he resumed his stage partnership with his wife under the name of 'The Elmas'. The success of their first tour under Harry Milne had not been forgotten and engagements were not slow to materialise. Harry Milne once paid Harry Gordon and Jose Goray the compliment that the two most successful acts on his books were The Elmas and the Fyffes - Will Fyffe and his wife. One of the features of their act was when Harry used to do lightning blackboard sketches while his wife danced. Songs derived from the popular Victorian music hall troupe, the Christy Minstrels, were also stable fare - and Harry actually revived one of his old minstrel songs for a broadcast in September, 1955. When the Elmas visited Kilsyth, Harry had written for the baggage man to meet him and on alighting from the train looked round for that official. Presently someone tapped him on the shoulder and asked,

"Wis ye lookin' for the baggage man?"

"Yes", Harry replied, "Where is he?"

"Ah'm him", he said, and promptly assisted Harry to take their cases along to the hall.

At the hall Harry asked him to take him to see the stage manager.

"Ah'm him", he replied.

"Good," said Harry, "Now I would like to see the electrician.".

"Ah'm him tae." he answered unperturbed.

Then Gordon inquired when the orchestra would be available to give them a run through their songs.

"It's only a piano", he replied, "But my son will be doon at five o'clock".

"That will suit", Harry replied, "And now I'll go upstairs and have a word or two with the manager".

"There's no need to go upstairs", said the other, "Ah'm him".

Duncan Wilson was the name of this supremo of the Kilsyth Hall and he was a great favourite with all the members of the theatrical profession who played in and around Glasgow.

A complete innovation was a show called 'Winners' which Harry Gordon, Jack Holden and Hugh Ogilvie, best remembered as the composer of 'Hail Caledonia' devised. It was conceived as a novel type of entertainment - a hybrid - something between a concert-party and a revue. The three just kept pegging away, writing the show at odd moments until they were satisfied with their material. They found, however, theatre managers - in general a conservative fraternity - very chary. Eventually, David Stewart, manager of the Clydebank Empire, agreed to give them a trial. Revue at that time was the popular craze, and 'Winners' was innovative within that tradition. Instead of about twenty to twenty-five people in the usual revue production they relied on a small but talented company of a dozen-eight principals and four dancers. There was no scenery, just draperies designed by Harry - cynically referred to as washing by some of the stage hands. However, the new ideas which they incorporated created as much favourable comment as they had hoped and the house was full every night. The cast of 'Winners' included in addition to the three who devised it, Jose Goray, whose singing and dancing were consistently praised and Doroswami, the violinist whose playing of "Home, Sweet Home" to his own piano accompaniment was regarded as especially clever. Items which later became part of Harry Gordon's standard repertoire such as 'Golf' with Jack Holden also appear in the programmes. Reference is made in many of the reviews not only to the individual quality of the artists but also to their teamwork.

'Winners' was a great success in Scotland, justifying the optimism with which the show had been launched. The first tour which extended over several months, ended happily at His Majesty's Theatre, Aberdeen, doing tremendous business. Indeed 'Winners' ran for nearly five years with breaks for pantomime.

It added to Harry Gordon's growing renown and enormously increased his market vale. All was set for the next phase of Harry Gordon's career. In 1924 'Winners' went to Ireland, but Harry did not go with them, for it was at that time, in conjunction with Cissy Murray, that he took over the Beach Pavilion, Aberdeen and all his energies were required there.

The late Victorian enthusiasm for beaches and their attendant attractions of bathing and sun-bathing made Aberdeen's sands an attractive proposition for the holiday maker. The coming of the railway had enabled the city to become readily accessible to the tourist. A smattering of bathing machines and some donkeys gradually appeared and eventually in 1896 a Bathing Station in baronial brick was erected to cope with the crowds. Aberdeen Beach, regardless of its often inhibiting North wind, had achieved popularity far beyond "twal' mil' roun". Entertainment began to be provided in the form of companies of pierrots - particuarly noteworthy were the Sinclairs, the Parrs and the Catlans. These troupes were comprised of local humorists - although for the sake of summer visitors, they learned to modify their dialect. In the absence of any cover, they had to perform in the open air. Aberdeen weather at the turn of the century was no different to what it is today, when rainstorms would quickly disperse patrons giving the unfortunate pierrot companies enforced half-holidays, with consequent loss of revenue.

Inevitably there was talk of providing covered accommodation for this light and airy form of seaside entertainment. So having decided that such a place of entertainment should be erected at the Beach, the Town Council approached David Thomson, the comedian, with the request that he should take the matter in hand. So it was that on the day of the May holiday 1905 the Aberdeen Beach Pavilion opened - a modest wooden building with a corrugated iron roof. The Council showed discernment in choosing David Thomson, for he had both the personality and business acumen to carry the scheme through to success. In this he was aided by his wife, Violet Davidson. In their hands the foundation of the Pavilion's fortunes were laid on safe and sure lines. In that era the Pavilion gave three performances daily, David Thomson being the Master of Ceremonies seated at the right hand side of the stage. The performing turns were, in general, descendents of the local pierrot tradition, but several performers who made their mark further afield also appeared. These included artists such as Daisy Taylor, Neil McKay and in 1921 Gertrude Lawrence, a young girl although already a star, along with Walter Williams.

Violet Davidson was herself one of the Pavilion's outstanding attractions. Violet, who had worked with Harry Lauder, was a brilliant concert soprano who imparted a great deal of sympathetic feeling into her songs. She is particuarly remembered for her singing of 'Hame o' Mine' which was composed by the famous Scottish violinist Mackenzie Murdoch. Years later, just before the Second World War, Violet reconstructed her old-time concert party for the B.B.C. under the title 'The North Stars'. Amongst these were Willie Johnson, a gentle tenor in the style of J. M.

Hamilton - a great favourite with Scots of a previous generation, comedians Dan Fraser and Danny Williams, Mr. and Mrs. Gus Stratton in domestic cross talk and the soubrette Juliette McLean.

Amongst David Thomson's promotional features at the pavilion were talent competitions which have remained a consistent feature of seaside entertainments ever since. It was in 1908 that a young Harry Gordon won one of these with the song 'Milk-O', appearing as a milkman with the traditional yoke over his shoulder.

Thereafter David Thomson followed his career with close interest and in 1913, Harry was offered his first engagement as a member of the Pavilion concert party. For his first week's work he received the sum of £2.00. One of David Thomson's likeable qualities was his ready wit. On one occasion Harry drew a black and white caricature of Thomson in evening dress, which he flattered himself, was very good. In due course Harry presented it to him with a self-satisfied "What do you think of that". After studying it long and earnestly he handed it back to him with the remark, "Ay, it's a fine suit!"

While Harry Gordon rapidly made a considerable name for himself at the Beach Pavilion, the First World War began to loom on the horizon. Curiously one of the first songs Harry sang at the Pavilion in 1913 was "It's a long way to Tipperary" and he sang it again in the Beach Pavilion in 1914 but under very different circumstances. War fever was abroad and the "contemptible little army" had already made the song famous. The Pavilion was commandeered by the military but their occupation lasted for only a week, after which David Thomson was able to resume his entertainments.

Harry's eyesight was so bad that he could not be accepted as a combatant soldier but in 1915, having attested under the 'Derby' scheme, he was first posted at Nigg in Ross-shire where he sang a number of concerts in the Y.M.C.A. hut; then to Blairgowrie and thence to France within five weeks of enlisting. Before leaving, Harry did manage to accept David Thomson's invitation to make a one-night appearance at the Pavilion. Although dressed in khaki, he looked anything but the pukka soldier, and probably for that very reason he received a hearty send off from the Pavilion audience.

Although non-combatant, Harry spent the next two and a half years almost constantly within the zone of fire and at one critical period of the war when he was stationed at Guiveres near Noyon he was issued with a rifle in preparation for taking his place in the trenches.

In order to relieve the monotony of life in camp, Harry recruited the services of some ten members of the company for a group of entertainers and formed his first concert party. Among them was Willie Smith, the Aberdeen baritone who had been in Harry's pierrot show at Banchory. Improvised concert items, character sketches with costumes from whatever material was available made up the programmes and, rough and ready as these entertainments were and often given in the open air, they became very popular and assisted in maintaining morale.

Immediately after the Armistice, Harry obtained his release from the army under somewhat peculiar circumstances. He was given Christmas leave and stepping off the train at Victoria Station, a military policeman buttonholed him. The police had orders to retain all men who had work to go to arranging for their immediate demobilisation. Seizing his opportunity, Harry said he had employment. A telegram to David Thomson brought the offer of an engagement. So it was that Harry Gordon was demobilised in three days and returned shortly afterwards to the Beach Pavilion.

Soon Harry Gordon not only took over as master of ceremonies, replacing David Thomson in the corner chair, but also gradually took over with Violet Davidson, the arrangement of programmes. David Thomson died in 1921 but Violet Davidson continued to run the Pavilion from 1921-1923. Harry Gordon missed the 1923 season but in 1924 he returned becoming lessee of the Pavilion in conjunction with Violet Davidson's niece, Mrs. Cissy Murray. Under their aegis 'Harry Gordon and his Entertainers' became a seaside show of growing renown, drawing loyal and enthusiastic crowds.

Harry was the driving force behind its success. He engaged the artists, designed the stage setting, produced and directed the show and wrote the programme for which he also designed the covers. In the 1920's, he produced some striking art nouveau designs incorporating the figures of Pierrot and Columbine. He prepared the press publicity material, always including a snappy line to catch the reader's attention. For the week of the "Glorious Twelfth" there was "Now the grouse season is on, Harry Gordon's Entertainers will make you forget all your worries" or the more general "Don't go near the Pavilion if you are afraid of laughing yourself to death". All this in addition to working on his own material, writing songs and preparing new comedy stunts and business. To those friends who supported him at the Beach Pavilion he promised, "You may always be sure of a clean healthy show and the best we can provide". Harry never told a joke which his public would find distasteful or smutty and he insisted on the same high standard from his visiting artists. Comedians with a predilection for the blue joke had their scripts inspected by Harry to ensure that their material did not transgress his own critical standards. Like Ben Popplewell who ran that great 'family' theatre, the Ayr Gaiety, Harry insisted on clean wholesome entertainment and this was a successful policy, not only artistically but commercially, ensuring continuing good business. A resident nucleus evolved - Harry Gordon, Jack Holden and Alice Stephenson.

Jack Holden is almost invariably associated with Harry Gordon although he did not work with him by any means for his entire career. They first met during an early pre-First World War tour when Harry Gordon was appearing with his wife as 'The Elma's in Fraserburgh. One night they noticed a stranger in stage make-up, standing in the wings watching their act and eating a bag of chips. After their turn was over, he introduced himself and the Gordons asked him into their dressing room where they helped him finish his chips. There were at that time two halls in Fraserburgh and Jack Holden had been booked to appear at the other hall. Struck by the small size of his audience he had asked the stage manager the reason, "Oh, the Elmas, Harry Gordon and his wife, ye ken, are at the other hall, and the crowd have gone to hear them" was the reply. "Who is this Harry Gordon?" Jack Holden asked and getting a vague and unsatisfactory reply he decided to see for himself. This was the beginning of what became a very happy and mutually profitable friendship. It would be wrong to say that they invariably exuded bonhomie off-stage, but professionally they worked together in the closest possible harmony.

Jack Holden was born in Forres and was brought up in Kirkcaldy in Fife. After that early meeting in Fraserburgh Jack and Harry worked together with Fred Collins troupe of pierrots at Burntisland in 1915. It was not however until after the Great War that their partnership really evolved. Jack worked mainly in the Glasgow area. He played the Lyric Theatre in Cathedral Street and the West End Playhouse (which became the Empress) where one of the first theatre organs in Scotland was installed - a great novelty. Jack also played the Savoy Theatre in Hope Street, running twice nightly variety with 22 acts on the bill - as one act went off another came on the opposite side. It was a short-lived experiment. In addition there was the Lyceum, Govan, with its 'tough' audience, the Gaiety, Anderston Cross; the Olympia, Bridgton; the Casino, Townhead; the Star, Partick and the more famous Panoptican in the Trongage with its four performances a day. As there were no shows in Glasgow during July and August, Jack spent the summers in the rough and tumble entertainment world of the Clyde resorts. These open-air shows were happy-go-lucky affairs with no script - the artists had to rely on their native wit - while the filling of the last collection box would signal the end of the sketch.

Jack Holden always liked Glasgow and enjoyed playing there - he was a great favourite later playing in the pantomime successes at the Pavilion, Alhambra and Theatre Royal.

13

After the First World War, Jack gradually appeared with increasing frequency at the old Aberdeen Beach Pavilion, his summer visits gradually lengthening from three to four weeks to cover the whole of the Summer season. Towards the end of the 1920's however, he did forsake the Pavilion for three seasons to work on his own - and a very good comic he was in his own right. One of the comedians who took his place was an up and coming artist, Jack Anthony, but by the early thirties Jack Holden was back in the fold. He had been connected with Harry in the show 'Winners' and in touring pantomime, and by the mid 1930's, the pair's professional association was complete and they worked together for the remainder of Jack's life. Holden died at the age of 62 in March 1955 at Elgin.

Jack was a brilliant comedy 'foil' or 'feed'. There was a certain element of physical contrast. In his younger days Holden dressed in a kilt could look like a highland athlete compared with the diminutive Harry Gordon. Physical contrast, as Laurel and Hardy and Abbot and Costello demonstrated, could be a useful comedy aside, but far more important in the case of Harry Gordon and Jack Holden was their brilliant comedy timing and their ability to dovetail their personalities together for theatrical efect. Sketches such as 'His Wedding Morn', 'Discord', 'The Welcome Stranger' relied on an exceptional rapport to be successful and that requirement was amply fulfilled. They wrote most of their own material and by the end of their careers possessed over 100 character duos. Much of the earlier material written in the Beach Pavilion days remained popular right through the '40's and into the '50's. Everything had been refined to perfection and the sketches were carried off with consummate artistry. Jack Holden also wrote the lyrics of several of Harry Gordon's song including 'The Inversnecky Scaffy', 'The Piper o' Deeside', 'The Village Baker', 'The Lawyer', 'The Railway Fireman', thus contributing to the advancement of Harry's career.

A most important figure at the Beach Pavilion was the pianist, Alice Stephenson. Her first appearance was in 1921 and she appeared in every subsequent summer season until the closure of the Pavilion in 1940. She accompanied all the performers, residents and guests with great accomplishment.

It was the flurry of creative activity which occurred in the years following 1925 - when a whole new range of Scots comic songs were being written by Archie Hyslop, Harry Gordon and Jack Holden which gave Alice Stephenson a new role - transcribing and harmonizing Gordon's original compositions. After writing the words of a song, Harry repeated them in his head until an appropriate tune evolved. He would then write it out in sol-fa then pick it out on the piano to make sure it was as he envisaged. The rough draft of the song was given to Alice Stephenson who wrote it down in staff notation - after which she provided the accompaniment. It was not uncommon for a song to be written on a Sunday night, transcribed and harmonized at rehearsal on the Monday morning, sung for the first time on the Monday night and broadcast throughout Scotland on the Tuesday.

Alice was a most thorough artist, taking great trouble to ensure that her accompaniments for the notable guest artists engaged in the 1930's could give no cause for complaint. On going to the Billy Mayerl School, that master of syncopation paid her the deserved compliment of saying that she was wasting her time there as he could not teach her anything she did not already know. Alice Stephenson also worked with Harry as musical director for some concert tours and pantomime. She subsequently became one of the pianists for that lively troupe 'The Fol-de-Rols'.

Alice Stephenson had a flat in Aberdeen at the top of what was then one of the highest properties in the city - in the tenement block over the Star and Garter Bar in Crown Street. Harry called to see her one day, toiled up the stairs and arriving at the top, he knocked on the door - his question on its being opened was 'Is God in?'".

One of the guest artists who figures prominently in the story of the old Beach Pavilion was Mackenzie Murdoch, the violinist who had worked with Harry Lauder. Mackenzie Murdoch was a great rival of the violinist who is still so revered, J. Scott Skinner, and Skinner would never play Murdoch's compositions nor Murdoch, Skinner's. A friend and admirer of both men, Harry Gordon was a pall-bearer at Scott Skinner's funeral in 1927. Murdoch was a great favourite with Beach Pavilion audiences and he was no less popular with the rest of the company as he was an attractive personality, and a considerable dressing room comedian. About the year 1920, Harry Gordon, Jack Holden and Mackenzie Murdoch started the practice of playing a round of golf every morning. They usually went at 7 o'clock or at 11 o'clock on the days there was no rehearsal. Mackenzie Murdoch was known as 'Mac' and his running comments of his own and the others's shots were considered extremely funny. His ideas of dress for the golf course were typical of his Bohemian spirit, playing without a collar or tie and with white tennis shoes. When he hit a good shot he would shout "Come away, Queen's Park" and when he duffed one he would inquire dolefully "Whit's wrang wi' Queen's Park the day?".

One day when they were playing at Balnagask a stranger asked him, "What is bogey here". "Threepence ha'penny an ounce". he replied.

Harry Gordon and Mackenzie Murdoch were once partners in a two ball foursome match against Jack Holden and another artist at the Aberdeen Links. At one hole, the fairway of which lies alongside the roadway, Harry struck a bad patch. He sliced his drive over the road into a field. Murdoch picked the ball out for two and Harry played again for the third shot. Twice again he sliced out of bounds, and Murdoch had to be content each time with picking the ball out and placing it on the fairway. Harry Gordon reached the green in seven but when everybody gathered there Murdoch hung back, apparently swithering as to what to do.

"Come on, Mac", said Holden, "Get a move on - it's your turn to play".

"That's just it," said Murdoch, "It's such a long time since I played golf, that I don't know what club to play".

Jack Holden and Harry Gordon incorporated many of Mackenzie Murdoch's comments in their sketch 'Golf'. With Jack as the golfer and Harry as the caddy this was one of the first double-act entertainments which they did together and it was very popular. It was played throughout the British Isles, was a successful gramophone record and was broadcast by the B.B.C. Later on, Harry did a character study 'The Inversnecky Golfer' the song itself written by Archie Hyslop in which Gordon's early experience obviously again proved a rich source of material for his patter.

Mackenzie Murdoch was an eccentric who had some curious foibles. His great ambition was to hear his popular song 'Hame o' Mine' played on the barrel organ. That he used to say, would be the height of fame for him. One day, after rehearsal some of the artists had repaired to the Saltoun Arms in Park Street, Aberdeen, Murdoch reading a newspaper while the others chatted. Suddenly he leaped from his chair and ran to the door - only then did the others realise that the familiar tune 'Hame o' Mine' was being played outside and, moveover, on a barrel organ. Mac handed a £1 note to the astonished organgrinder and returning to the bar, called for drinks all round, "I'm famous at last" - he said by way of explanation.

Another artist whose performances were a source of never-failing pleasure to the Beach Pavilion for many years was Percy Forde, a brilliant female impersonator. 'The Perfect Lady' as he was known, designed and made all his dresses and was often more up-to-date in his ideas than the ladies of the company, known for their keen fashion sense. His make-up, like his costuming, was meticulous and while he had many tricks played on him by the cast he took it all in good part. Harry Gordon learned a great deal about the art of female impersonation from Percy Forde which he applied in his own dame studies. Forde whose real name was John Wright, died in 1970 aged eighty-two.

Amongst the many other artists who appeared at the old Beach Pavilion were Laurence Hepworth - the baritone whose rendering of 'The Volga Boat Song' was one of his popular numbers, Micky Francis, Elliot Dobie - the eminent bass who was Robert Wilson's first singing teacher and Winnie Braemar.

Behind the success story of the Beach Pavilion in the 1920's was the hard work and enterprise of Harry Gordon himself. Mrs. Cissy Murray looked after the business side of the concern, but Harry dealt with most of the other aspects of running the theatre in addition to preparing his own songs and comic materials.

Such was the success of Harry Gordon's Summer Seasons that in the late 1920's the Town Council decided to replace the old wooden Pavilion which had given valiant service for twenty-two summer seasons. And so in 1928 a new Beach Pavilion - a theatre of delightful intimacy - was opened and with it a further chapter in the successful story of 'Harry Gordon and his Entertainers' was about to begin.

4. THE MAN FROM INVERSNECKY

Harry Gordon was a great admirer of Sir Harry Lauder. He once said in a broadcast "We Scots comedians should always play the game of follow the leader - and that leader of course is Sir Harry Lauder whose clean and healthy humour together with his other wonderful talents enabled him to become the greatest variety star the world has ever known". Harry Gordon started early in his footsteps in that one of the first songs he ever sang was 'I'm the saftest o' the family'. During the Beach Pavilion era Harry Gordon was very proud of the fact that Lauder would often visit those summer shows when in Aberdeen playing His Majesty's Theatre and Gordon was charmed when he shared the same dressing room as Lauder at a charity matinee at the Glasgow Empire in 1932. Indeed, Gordon used to do impressions of Lauder, inevitably caricaturing the famous 'wiggle, wiggle, waggle o' the kilt'. It would be a mistake however, to say that Gordon's style owed a great deal to the Lauder tradition, apart from a few songs such as 'The Lassie that I love so well' and 'The lass I'm Courtin Noo', sung by Gordon in the vigorous manner of Lauder's famous, if somewhat tasteless, song 'I love a lassie'. Lauder's was very much a solo act, whereas Harry Gordon's repertoire embraced solo songs and character studies, comedy duos as well as larger production numbers. Lauder could hardly be called a flexible artist - he was a 'Scotch comedian' whose image was based on the wearing of the kilt and a repertoire limited by that image. Gordon, off stage, wore the kilt with pride and on stage on occasions much as the 'Half-Past Eight' finales, but there was no suggestion of the 'guying' of the kilt, a charge sometimes levelled at Lauder by his detractors.

There was no theatrical background in Harry Gordon's family so that he learned the profession from scratch through his own successes and failures. The opportunities to do this through pierrot troupe and concert party work existed in a way that they do not in the North-east today. That he survived the system and went on to greater things was the result of his own hard work and talent. Gordon however, did not really find his true style - that which was to suit him for the rest of his life, until the mid 1920's.

When he first appeared on the stage there was a wealth of published music hall songs, so this was on aspect of the comedian's profession which caused him no concern. Not only had he not to bother about writing his own material, but he did not have to worry about the question of buying the sole rights in any particular composition that might take his fancy. However, by the early 1920's, this supply of new material had virtually dried up. The Golden Age of the music hall had passed with the First World War- business had been very difficult during the abnormal circumstances caused by the war and the 'new-fangled' motion pictures, although lacking both sound and colour, were beoming more competitive. With the decline of the music hall, so also came the inevitable decline in the supply of music hall songs. Thus, for better or for worse, the individual comedian was thrown back on his own resources, a circumstance which weeded out some of the less imaginative members of the profession at the time.

Until the mid 1920's, Harry Gordon's repertoire consisted of songs of the broad comedy type, all of them of English origin - songs such as 'Dandelions and Daffodils', 'The Road Hog's in Town', and 'She seems to know'. However the growing lack of suitable material forced Gordon to look for alternative sources and it was at this time that a happy occurence took place which led to the birth of a whole new range of Scots comic songs and also to the creation of 'Inversnecky'.

It was towards the end of the 1925 summer season at the Aberdeen Beach Pavilion that a gentleman came to Harry and diffidently asked him to hear a little song written in the Aberdeen dialect which he thought might suit him. Harry was so taken with the song when he tried it through that he agreed to sing it at the next performance. He did and it was an instantaneous success. A local newspaper reported 'Mr. Harry Gordon excelled himself at the Beach Pavilion last night, with his humorous burlesque 'She Dee't', every verse of the song giving rise to outbursts of laughter. This is likely to rank as one of Mr. Gordon's most successful ditties - a masterpiece of mirth'.

SHE DEE'T

1.   Puir auld Mistress Murphy, she wis turnin' ninety-twa;
    She snuffed an' chewed tobacca wi' the best amang them a';
    She'd hid a cauld for forty years an' aye hid warstled wi't.
    An' fit dae ye think she did last week? She dee't.

2.   Puir auld Mistress Mackintoddle, she wis auld as weel;
    But 'Hooch' says Mistress Mackintoddle, 'I'm as auld's as I feel'.
    She went an' ate a partin though the kent it widna gree.
    An' fit dae ye think she did last week? She dee't tee.

3.   Puir auld Mistress Malcolm said that life wis full o' woe,
    An' frae this vale o' vanity she'd no be sweer to go.
    Through her nesty tonge wi' a' her neebours she hid striven;
    An fit d'ye think's become o' her? She's aye livin'.

4.   Willie wis a fitba fiend; he played frae morn till nicht.
    The doctor sounded Willie, found his heart wis far frae richt.
    He said 'Ye've kicked yer final kick; ma lad, ye'll hae tae chuck it.'
    But Willie's proved the doctor wrang - he's kicked the bucket.

5.   Puir auld Mistress Mellinsfodder dearly loved a toot;
        Ae nicht an overdose o' gin an' bitters laid her oot.
        Her spiritualistic freens begood to find the climate she's in
        D'ye ken the state they foond her in? .... Bleezin

The author of 'She dee't' and subsequently of many of Gordon's best known songs insisted on remaining anonymous. He used several pen names, many of which derived from Scottish place names and humorous corrupted versions. Included amongst these were Forbes Hazelwood (the surname a combination of two adjacent Aberdeen districts, Hazlehead and Woodend), Rae Elrick, Steven Hive (a reference to the common North East pronounciation of Stonehaven). Behind these pseudonyms was Dr. Archibald Forbes Hyslop, an Aberdonian, a distinguished scholar who was a teacher of English and Latin from 1921 until 1924 at Aberdeen Grammar School, taking up a further appointment at Manchester Grammar School and subsequently returning to Scotland in 1928 as one of H. M. Inspectors of Schools. Before 1925 he had been the successful author, with Eric Linklater, of a student charity show and had contributed comic sketches to the 'London Opinion' and for no less a magazine than 'Punch'. He also wrote a Scout opera.

'She Dee't' was the beginning of a successful and happy partnership between Harry Gordon and Archie Hyslop. Hyslop wrote the lyrics and music which often contained many subtle satricial touches while Gordon contributed the patter. Archie Hyslop wrote and composed such songs as 'The Ghost o' Mistress McIntyre', 'A Tattie, a Neep and an Ingen', 'The story that I startit at the Kirk soiree', 'The Beadle o' the Kirk' and 'A song of Cove', recalling the days of the old fish meal factory with its incredible smell.

        'Now nae sae very lang ago, I dreamed that I was deid
        And Auld Nick cam' to meet me wi' the horns upon his heid.
        He says 'We've been expecting ye, jist come awa' inside'
        But fin I saw my rooms I said 'If this is faur I've tae bide - oh
        Tak' me back tae Cove, tak' me back tae Cove
        Faur the air is as strong as can be.
        Auld Nick says 'Please yersel' but I couldna stand yon smell
        By the side o' the silvery sea'.

There was also 'Sing me a Hebridean Song' parodying the Hebridean folk-song, which was then enjoying a considerable vogue through the researches and innumerable performances of Marjorie and Patuffa Kennedy-Fraser while Sir Hugh Roberton's 'Songs of the Isles' had, with his Glasgow Orpheus Choir, given a popular slant to the cultivation of choral music.

Harry Gordon's Hebridean plaint runs thus -

> 'I am sad and weary, Very far frae cheery,
> Sing an eerie, dreary song
> that makes your optic bleary.
> Fill me fou o' sorrow, From the Gaelic borrow
> The sort o' lay that starts today an' goes on till tomorrow'.

One of the recurring themes in Scottish humour is laughing at the macabre. In literary terms, there is Robert Louis Stevenson's humorous novel 'The Wrong Box' which centres on a corpse deposited in a grand piano. On the variety stage there is a sketch which Rikki Fulton used to do at the Edinburgh Gateway. Fulton visiting a friend in hospital fired off a barrage of jokes such as "This'll be an awkward kind of place to get a coffin out of". This sketch was strangely reminiscent of Harry Gordon and Arthur Black's gramophone record 'Mrs. McIntyre visits the sick'. The humorous reaction to fear of the unknown is exemplified in another Harry Gordon number which was a great favourite, Archie Hyslop's 'Fine Man, John'.

> Oh' a fine man John - aye anither man gone;
> Anither for the daisies an' the grass to grow upon
> He wis an elder o' the kirk respeckit an' sedate
> He workit in its interests frae early morn till late
> But there aye wis a defeecit fan he chaperoned the plate,
> Oh a fine man John, aye a gran' man John.

Some enthusiasts have described 'The Auldest Aiberdonian', one of the earliest Hyslop numbers appearing just after 'She dee't' as in the immortal category and it is certainly a marvellously funny song, full of local allusions with a catchy tune and put over by Harry Gordon in brilliant fashion. Verses 1, 2, 3, 4, 5 and Chorus run:

THE AULDEST AIBERDONIAN

1. I'm the auldest man that's every lived in Aiberdeen,
   Lots and lots of famous things and people I hae seen.
   I can min' when Wallace in this city spent an 'oor;
   I went an' hid a drink wi' him inside the Wallace Toor.

   CHORUS: Fittie fawk, Kitty fawk, country folk and city fawk,
   Fawk fae Constitution Street and folk fae Rubislaw Den,
   Wallfield, Nellfield, Mannofield an' Cattofield,
   List to local stories that professors dinna ken.

21

2. I can min' fin Bruce the great King Robert - cam' by here.
    The Council held a banquet; aye the rates went up that year.
    They thankit Bruce for keepin' a' the English oot o' reach
    Ye see it hidna struck us then to advertise the beach.

    CHORUS: (Last line: List to local stories Dr. Bulloch disna ken)

3. I can min' fin Shakespeare acted in a traivellin' show,
    They chairged ye for admission;so of course I didna go,
    I min' Henry VIII arrivin' in his royal gig,
    And caravans wi' Henry's wives stretched a' the wye to Nigg.

    CHORUS: (Last line: List to local stories G. M. Fraser disna ken)

4. I can min' on Hazleheid afore there wis a tram.
    I can min' when Mr. Walker first said Walker's Dam.
    I can mind when fo.lks wis hangt beside the Mercat Cross,
    And I can min' fin there wis peacocks doon in Peacock's Close.

    CHORUS: (Last line: List to local stories Jimmy Taggart disna ken)

5. I can min' afore the perfume factiry cam' to Cove
    I can min' the time there wis nae bairns in Union Grove,
    Lots o' ither things I'd min' if I had time to think
    But I canna min' fin anybody offered me a drink.

    CHORUS: (Last line: I could keep ye listenin' if ye hadna tae ging hame)

    CHORUS: (2nd time)
            Fittie fawk, Kitty fawk, country fawk and city fawk,
            Fawk fae Constitution Street and fawk fae Persley Den,
            Rubislaw, Pointlaw, Cairncraw and Babbie Law
            Naething every happens that this youngster disna ken.

The rousing chorus was designed for Aberdonian audience participation.

Cuthbert Graham, the distinguished Aberdeen journalist, opined in an article 'The Humour of Aberdeen' that "it is not perhaps too much to say that in singing the Harry Gordon choruses Aberdonians felt, perhaps for the last time, a sense of total involvement with the identity of their ever-expanding city".

For the 1929 pantomime 'The Queen of Hearts' in Edinburgh, Harry Gordon altered the words and it became 'The Auldest Dame in Edinburgh' - and it was a great hit there also. Hyslop was also responsible for other pantomime numbers appropriate to the Scottish city in which Harry was appearing such as 'When The Broom Blooms Bricht On The Bonnie Broomielaw' for Glasgow - 'Where Is My Wandering Boy Today' and 'Princes Street' for Edinburgh.

Hyslop wrote for Harry Gordon for most of the rest of his life. He wrote the special song for Gordon's appearance at the Glasgow Empire Exhibition in May 1938 and also contributed numbers for his Glasgow Alhambra pantomimes early in the Second World War. In addition to his writing for Harry Gordon, Hyslop also contributed radio sketches for the Aberdeen studios in Belmont Street and later for the B.B.C. in Glasgow.

Hyslop died after a swift and unexpected illness in 1943, at a time when, in addition to his considerable duties as an Inspector of Schools, he was also chairman of the Scottish Co-ordinating Committee of the Council for the Encouragement of Music and the Arts and had been using his talents as a script and song writer for E.N.S.A. (Entertainment National Services Association). As Arthur Black later recalled, Harry Gordon never forgot his debt to Archie Hyslop.

Harry Gordon also started writing his own material in the mid 1920's with songs such as 'A Limb O' The Law', 'The Society Man', 'The Rodin Tree' and 'Hilly's Man'.

HILLY'S MAN

I'm foreman at Hilly's, first horseman as weel,
An' I got this job when I left aff th' schule,
I'm foreman an' strapper an' orra man tae,
Cos Hilly has only ae man an' that's me.

There's tatties tae lift, and there's neeps to be pu'ed,
Kye tae be milk-it, and fields tae be plooed
There's plently tae dae up at Hilly's ye see,
Cos Hilly has only ae man an' that's me.

There's a ball on next Friday am' A'm takin' Jean,
A quine in the kitchen, a guid lookin' deem;
I'll buy 'conversations' and try her wi that,
For I'm thinkin' I'll maybe try an' hing up ma hat.

She's a grand hand at sowens and skilly forebye,
she can mak' chapped tatties, an' whiles shepherd's pie;
Oh, there's plenty tae dae up at Hilly's ye see,
For Hilly has only ae man, an' that's me.

The patter is quoted here as a typical example of the twenties style and accords with his usual procedure.

Ye've never been up at Hilly's hev ye? A great muckle lump a' grun' yonder. A most commodious tract o' vegetation altogether. It takes me aboot three days to walk roon' about it on a bicycle.

Oh, an' ye've never met Jean. That's the kitchen lassie. What a worker! She flies aboot the hoose like a traction engine. Sometimes she has the beds made afore we're up. An' what a cook! What you would call rough an' ready. Her meals are aye rought, but never ready. A sort of religious cook - everything she serves up is either a sacrifice or a burnt offering.

An' ye've never met Hilly. A fine man, but awfu' pernickety. I was paintin' the barn the ither day, and he said tae me. 'Now, mak' a good job o't, an' put on three coats.' Speak about being suffocated. I'd tae tak' off two o' them, as it wis just a bit too warm.

We're haein' an awfu' time o' rain. A' oor grun's under water. I doot if Hilly was going to seel the farm noo. he wouldna' know whether tae sell it by the yaird of by the pint! Well, I doot I'll hae tae be knypin' on for -

There's tatties tae lift, and there's neeps tae be pu'ed,
Kye tae be milk-it, and fields tae be plooed
There's plenty tae dae up at Hilly's ye see,
Cos Hilly has only ae man an' that's me.

The references here to farming life were widely appreciated in the urban setting of Aberdeen at a time when the rising population of the town was still being fed by immigrants from the rural hinterland - they would have been meaningless in a wholly industrial community. And songs such as 'Hilly's Man' with particulary regional propensities did not survive the 1930's which saw the increasing standardization of ways of life.

It was against this background that 'Inversnecky' came into being, a fictitious village peopled with characters and institutions which all Aberdonians could recognise as typical of the small village in the North East. Who actually invented Inversnecky is not clear. Harry Gordon used to relate the story that in one of his travelling pantomime companies was an Aberdeen girl who had a way of expressing herself which he thought very singular. When describing herself walking she would make a characteristic wriggling movement with her arms and say "I just went snakin' along". The word 'snaking' stuck in Gordon's mind striking him as being particularly expressive. In his own mind he called the girl 'snaky' and from there it was quite an easy transition to 'Inversnecky'. Inversnecky was certainly put on the map of Scottish entertainment and the mystery of its location was cleared up by Harry Gordon himself at a luncheon address in Aberdeen many years later.

"Ye gang oot there for sixteen miles", he said pointing in the direction of Deeside/Donside, "and ye come to a signpost. On ae side it says 'You are just entering Inversnecky and on the ither you are just leaving Inversnecky'. It takes ye an oor by train fae Aberdeen, an oor an' a half by bus, an' if you wait for a lift it micht take a lifetime!"

The song 'The Invesnecky Bus' provides a further clue:

'Aiberdeen tae Inversnecky and Inversnecky back tae Aiberdeen
I go up and doon the stairs collecting a' the fares
Watching a' the spoony couples sitting there in pairs.
First stop's the Mill Inn
then the Brig o' Feugh,
The bus is very comfy though it's shaky,
And if the driver canna see, gings off the road and hits a tree
When you come down, ye'll maybe land in Inversnecky'

Inversnecky, like Brigadoon, has now almost faded into the mists of time. There are few reminders today of the village that a generation of Aberdonians once knew better than their own neighbourhood and of the characters which kept them laughing. Visitors to the city were frequently amazed to learn that there was no such place such was its fame among Scotsmen at home and abroad.

The very first Inversnecky number was 'The Barber' written by Archie Hyslop in which Inversnecky appeared only in the patter which was written by Harry Gordon himself. Other 'Inversnecky' songs written by Archie Hyslop show the extraordinary compatibility of writer and performer. These include 'The Bells of Inversnecky'.

THE BELLS OF INVERSNECKY

Ding, dong, goes the bell in ilka steeple,
A simultaneous broadcast in every kind o' key.
Hark at them - a-calling to the people,
To the shepherd on the mountainside, the sailor on the sea.
They reach the landlord o' the pub and gie him cause to think,
He vows nae mair the laws o' licen'in he'll try to jink
Then he pulls down the blinds and serves the bobby wi' a drink,
At Inversnecky, on a Sunday mornin'.

The Bells o' Inversnecky ring
Upon a Sunday morning
Eh-my - we're awfy late the day,
Bringing tae the countryside
Encouragement and warnin',
Hiv ye got the pandrops, it's time we were away.
Some gie oot a cheerfu' soun' and some a dismal toll,
Maist o' them are crackit, just a few o' them are whole,
Some min you' on funerals, and ithers upon coal
At Inversnecky on a Sunday mornin'.

Ding, dong goes the bell in ilka steeple,
A simultaneous broadcast in every kind o' key.
Hark at them - a calling to the people,
To the shepherd on the mountainside, the sailor on the sea.
The lawyer hears them, busy at conveyencin' and wills.
It wakens up his conscience and his eyes a tear-drop fills,
And his han' it shaks so much, it adds ten pounds to a' the bills.
At Inversnecky on a Sunday morning.

PATTER
But isn't it fine to be wakened up on a Sunday mornin' by the Kirk bells
ringing, telling ye that the 'News of the World' has arrived and then ye
ken ye can lie in yer bed until denner-time? It's great isn't it? A man
came up to me the ither day and asked me 'Why are the bells ringin'?' I
said 'Because I'm pullin' the ropes.' Last Sunday I was ringing' for
three hours and when I got ootside it was pourin' hail water and when
I got home I was still wringin'. And I found out that I had knockit my
wrist oot. I saw the doctor-mannie and he rubbit on some o' yon Sloan's

linoleum and said it would seen be better. I said, "When it's better will
I be able to play the melodeon?" He said, "Surely, surely." I said, "Man
that's wonderful, I could never play it afore". But there's nothing beats
the bells especially on a Sunday morning when -

Ding, dong, goes the bell in ilka steeple, ˜
A simultaneous broadcast in every kind o' key.
Hark at them - a calling to the people,
To the sailor on the mountainside, the shepherd on the sea.
The milkman hears their music, in his throat there comes a lump,
The tears fa' doon his cheeks and tae his milk gang wi' a plump,
But he lets them fa' awa' and saves a journey tae the pump,
At Inversnecky on a Sunday mornin'.

Other Hyslop 'Inversnecky' numbers included 'Inversnecky Lasses', Inversnecky
Anthem', 'Inversnecky Golfer', 'Inversnecky Pub', 'Inversnecky Art Gallery' and the
tremendously popular 'The Billposter.'

THE INVERSNECKY BILLPOSTER

I've posted bills in Inversnecky too for mony a year,
And that's been my profession since my youth,
And I've never felt distaste for my brushie and my paste,
While advertisin' still stuck tae the truth.
But since Inversnecky started boomin' as a waterin' place,
I feel my reputation's gone, my work I canna face
When I regard the bills I stick I feel no better than
A parliamentary candidate or a patent-medicine man,
For it's - 'Come tae Inversnecky when the bloom is on the heather,
And the sheep are at the shearin' ere the summer days have ceased'
Aye - and when yer bill is reckoned
You'll fin' oot in half a second,
That it's nae the sheep alone in Inversnecky that are fleeced.

PATTER
Aye, I've been sticking' up bills noo for over twenty years. I've stuck up
so mony I'm beginnin' to feel stuck up mysel'. It was all right till the new
bills cam' oot - Ye ken the kind - 'See Inversnecky and die happy'. Man o'
man, if you stoppit here mair than a week you'd be glad to die happy or no
happy. You've never been there, have you? Oh, dear, dear. When you come

oot o' the station you've aboot twa mile to walk to the village. We tried to
mak' it shorter. We pit the milestanes closer the gither but it was jist as
lang. Well, efter ye leave the station when ye get to the top o' the hill ye
get a fine view o' the village. That's of course if there's no a coo standin'
in front o' it. We've no skyscrapers. Oh oor sky disna need scrapin' - it
needs a sheet o' blottin' paper. And the wind usually blows frae the South.
If it ever blows frae the North, we ken it's just the South wind comin' back
again. Oh it's a great place - to be oot o'. Look at this poster - 'Spend yer
holidays in Inversnecky'. Dear me when we dive get ony visitors that's
about a' they do spend - their holidays. And here's anither poster -
The view o' Inversnecky wi the sky a brilliant blue,
But a cry o' protest bursts frae oot my lips,
For we hivna seen the sun since 1891,
And then it was a partial eclipse.
And the picture o' Glen Snecky wi' the burnie running' through.
On its wey to the distillery to be turned to mountain dew.
It's far ower black tae sparkle that's the mystery o' the matter,
For the water looks like porter and the whisky tastes like water.
And it's - 'Come to Inversnecky when the bloom is on the heather,
And the maidens pass demurely, oh so simple and so young,
And the lark in heaven is singin'.
and the bee wi' honey's wingin'.
And you're lucky if it's only by a bee that yet get stung.

'Inversnecky' numbers also flowed from the pens of Harry Gordon himself including
'The Smith of Inversnecky', 'The Inversnecky Doctor' and the 'Inversnecky Fireman'
with its racy patter.

Oh, dear me, there's that phone again - ah'll hae to be - jist a minute then -
I'll be ower to you in half a second ..... Aye? Hello! Fire Station
speaking....yes...yes...What? Who's a liar? - Oh a fire - oh - aye. Oh no,
but we canna come the day no, no, this is oor half holiday the day ye see.
Aye. Oh no, no, the horses are awa' to a funeral and I dinna ken whit
time they'll be back at. No, no. It's a peety ye didna ring up yesterday,
mm, mm, aye, we might have arranged something ye see. You couldna
keep it going until the morn's morning, could ye? Oh maybe. Whit is it?
Aye: one o' the new council hooses; man o' man, they winna burn, min -
no, no, - it must be the man next door lighting his pipe and you're seeing
the reflection through the wa'. Aye. What? It's bleezin. Eh? Oh, you
are. Oh, I see. Is there a lot o' smoke? Much? Aye, Ye hivna got a drop

o' petrol lying roon about have you, then we could come roon' and see
you the morn's morning, jist after breakfast time; aye, maybe in time for
a fly cup, one never knows. Well, well, we'll see you: oh no, I hope it
disna rain, that would spoil it, wouldn't it.

Jack Holden also contributed several lyrics - 'The Inversnecky Scaffy', for example
for which Harry Gordon wrote the music.

THE INVERSNECKY SCAFFY

By profession I'm a scaffy, so I'm always in the soup,
I've also got a brother that's a sweep.
I'm an artist with my little brush, altho' I canna paint.
My accomplishments have put the rest to sleep.
To carry out a job like mine, you must have inspiration,
I'm the cleansing department of the 'Snecky corporation.

CHORUS: Sweep, sweep, sweep, sweep, up and doon the toon,
               Early ev'ry mornin' you'll see me on my roon,
               Me and the barrow, the shovel and the brush,
               Whistling like a linty, singing like a thrush.
               My red letter day, is a Seterday,
               Because it is the day I get my 'haffie'
               Sunday mornin' in the rain,
               oot comes the brush again,
               It's a terrible awful affie job a scaffie.

Now for a scaf-in-geer, the winter tim'es the worst.
'Cos that's the season when we get the sna'.
The shovel's workin' overtime, the barrow's always fu',
I often feel like gettin' fu' an' a'.
An' yet I mustn't say a word against my freends sae trusty,
It'll be a blue look oot for me, the day my shovel's rusty.

PATTER
You know, I wisna born wi' a silver spoon in ma mooth - it must have
been a barra. And look at this brush, it's wonderful! I've painted wi' it;
I've whitewashed the roof wi' it; I've even shaved wi' it! And what an
artist I am wi' it, too! I can sweep a pile o' dust from Peebles to Perth
without losing a drop! See me sweepin' up confetti. One flick o' the brush

and it's in the barra.. There was a very posh wedding the other day, and they cut up stamps to make confetti. Of course it had to rain, and I'd tae pick up each bit separately! The other day I wis emptyin' the dustbins in the West End, and I got into an awfu' row fae a man just because I'd emptied his baby car by mistake. Well, it wis startin' there along wi' the ither buckets! One day I saw a threepenny bit lying in the middle o' the road, and do you know I swept that threepenny bit for three miles before I got a chance tae pick it up? Ah, well, maybe one day I'll be lucky in a

> CHORUS: Sweep, sweep, sweep, sweep, up and doon' the toon,
> Early every mornin' you'll see me on my roon,
> Me and the barrow, the shovel and the brush,
> Whistlin' like a linty, singing like a thrush.
> My red letter day s a Seterday,
> Because it is the day I get my 'haffie'
> Sunday mornin' in the rain,
> oot comes the brush again,
> It's a terrible awful affie job a scaffie.

In addition to his Inversnecky numbers, popular song parodies were an essential part of Harry Gordon's repertoire. When the blues were all the rage - the 'St. Louis Blues', 'Basin Street Blues', Harry Gordon had 'Boardin' Hoose Blues' particularly appropriate for the Aberdeen holiday season - and 'Drambuie Blues'.

> CHORUS: Sweep, sweep, sweep, sweep, up and doon' the toon,
> Early every mornin' you'll see me on my roon,
> Me and the barrow, the shovel and the brush,
> Whistlin' like a linty, singing like a thrush.
> My red letter day s a Seterday,
> Because it is the day I get my 'haffie'
> Sunday mornin' in the rain,
> oot comes the brush again,
> It's a terrible awful affie job a scaffie.

In addition to his Inversnecky numbers, popular song parodies were an essential part of Harry Gordon's repertoire. When the blues were all the rage - the 'St. Louis Blues', 'Basin Street Blues', Harry Gordon had 'Boardin' Hoose Blues' particularly appropriate for the Aberdeen holiday season - and 'Drambuie Blues'.

> 'Oh I've got the dram, I've got the dram Drambuie Blues,

When you are asked to have one, no option ye can choose
It's in the rules of etiquette that you must not refuse
I so I tak' a dram, I tak' the dram Drambuie booze.

Then there was that popular dance, the Carriocha and Harry Gordon's version -

'I want to do the Carriocha
And see my auntie doon in Yoker
She'll give me mince and tapioca'.

There also also an 'Inversnecky Moon' an Archie Hyslop composition, based on the popular 'Carolina Moon'.

This material provided the fullest scope for Harry Gordon's character interpretations. One very popular number 'The Auldest Student' found him dressed up with a long white flowing beard and 'a penny for ma piece'. He was also excellent as the Provost and the Photographer when he appeared with a huge ancient box camera, big black cloth and the 'birdie' which popped up when he had released the shutter.

'Moisten the lips wi' the pointie o' the tongue,
Dinna look as if ye were expectin' tae be hung,
Try and wear a pleasant smile if that be in your power,
And watch for the birdie and the hale thing's ower'.

In addition to these comedy miniatures there were extended numbers such as 'The Call o' the Hielans', which incorporated various elements of rousing chorus, descriptive passages, satire, straight comedy with a little sentiment thrown in for good measure. In 'The Call o' the Heilans' the North-East bothy ballads purveyed by Willie Kemp are satirized,

'As I cam' ower by Skirlie Neuk, upon a day t'fee
I met in wi' a tinker sittin' makin' tea,
I says "You'll hae to move man, you have nae business here"
He says I hivna got a spoon and so I canna steer.'

Harry Gordon was never happier than when in costume for a character part, although he was never the character actor that Will Fyffe or Jack Radcliffe at their best could be - Harry Gordon's sketches never went so far as Jack Radcliffe's as a drunken beachcomber in which the histrionics became melodramatic self-indulgence.

31

However, Gordon could use the contrast of sentiment as in his extended number 'The Piper o' Deeside'. Harry Gordon had within a few years from the mid 1920's established a whole new repertoire of original material which became the basis of his act for the remainder of his career. Even in the 1930's however, Harry Gordon's material was not exclusively Scottish. One song for which he was widely known south of the Border was the very English 'Hang 'em out on the old washing line' by Ralph Stanley and Jay Whidden.

Also of considerable importance were the comedy duos which Gordon evolved with Jack Holden and which are discussed more fully elsewhere.

Harry Gordon's dialect was that of urban Aberdeen and strong though it seems on rehearsing broadcasts from the Aberdeen Beach Pavilion, he was nevertheless perfectly comprehensible to the far wider radio audiences shown conclusively by the nationwide popularity of these broadcasts in the 1930's. It is noteworthy, however, that his accent became less strong when he became established in Glasgow and Edinburgh.

Of the characteristics of his performance, first and foremost must rank his verbal brilliance. He could speak articulately and fluently yet still have a superb sense of comedy timing. Jimmy Jogan who worked with Harry gordon in 'Half-Past Eight' and pantomime called him, "an instinctively funny man, who knew exactly the pulse of North-East audiences. He was exceptionally clever with words and was what I'd call a whiplash comedian. Harry could tell twice as many jokes as any other comedian in the same time.

Also important in Harry Gordon's presentation of his act was his attention to detail. Costumes had to be perfect and all details of 'props' absolutely correct. Gordon's aim was for a show suitable for all the family with an insistence on clean and wholesome material. As such he never told a smutty or hurtful joke on stage and by the same token insisted that no one else on the bill did.

He was once conducting auditions for prospective artists and after listening to one comedian he stopped him after his first song.

"No, I'm afraid your style and material wouldn't suite me. I can't allow any profanity at the Pavilion, Aberdeen," he said.

"But I don't use any profanity" was the indignant reply.

"No," said Harry, blowing away a puff of Churchman's No. 1, "but by Jingo - the audience would! .... Cold today!"

"SAMMY TAKES THE CAKE"

1.   Harry (second from the left, back row) and Jack Holden (standing extreme right) worked together with Fred Collins Pierrots at Burntisland, Fife in 1915.

2. A typical Beach Pavilion programme cover design, 1924. - All done by the talented Mr. Gordon.

3. Shop scene in Dick Whittington Pantomime at His Majesty's Theatre, Aberdeen, December 1927. On steps - Harry Gordon; in front of counter (left to right), Jack Fraser, Ellis Drake, and Jack Anthony.

4. On stage at the Beach Pavilion, 1929. The Company included: Herbert Cameron, Dunn and Dee, J. E. Sutton, Alice Stephenson, Micky Francis, Ray Cardle, the Three Gordon Girls, Vera Siddons, and "himself".

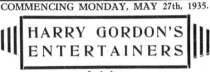
5.   The Pavilion continued to feature big name acts throughout the 20's and 30's. On this occasion, the celebrated "Mr." Floatsam" and "Mr. Jetsam" provided 'Songs at the Piano'.

ABERDEEN BON-ACCORD AN' NORTHERN PICTORIAL. Aberdeen, Saturday, November 2, 1929.

COAL!

Screened English Household
from 34/- per ton.
JOHN LEWIS Ltd
188 Albert Quay, ABERDEEN.
Telephone No. 847 & 3188.
"Grams: "Boiler, Aberdeen."

FIREWOOD
Thoroughly Seasoned and Dry
KINDLING 2/-
BLOCKS 2 6
CHARLES LYON,
LTD.
N. ESPLANADE
Phone 275

Aberdeen Bon-Accord
and Northern Pictorial.
THE WEEK-END FAMILY JOURNAL IN ABERDEEN, BANFF, MORAY, AND KINCARDINE.
WITH WHICH IS INCORPORATED "THE BAILIE."

NEW SERIES No. 188.   [REGISTERED AT THE GENERAL / POST OFFICE AS A NEWSPAPER]   SATURDAY, NOVEMBER 2, 1929.   BORN 1880.   PRICE, TWOPENCE.

GREAT FIRST NIGHT FOR ABERDONIANS: HARRY GORDON AT LONDON PALLADIUM

"FITTIE FOWK .... KITTIE FOWK .... COUNTRY FOWK AN' CITY FOWK ....

FOWKS FAE CONSTITUTION STREET, AN' FOWKS FAE RUB'SLAW DEN ...."

TAE LONDON TOWN THEY TRAVELLED BY "THE INVERSNECKY EXPRESS."

6.   "If I telephone at midnight", said Harry before he left, "you'll know I've clicked all right, so dinna bother answering the phone, then I'll nae hiv tae pay the call."

7.   A rare interior illustration of the Pavilion, 1929. Harry is seen here accepting one of the many gifts presented to him by an adoring public - usually, at the end of the season.

The Man fra' Inversnecky.

HARRY GORDON

Some Real Laughter Makers.

R 479 { A Fine Man John.
{ The Inversnecky Fireman.

R 480 { The Bells of Inversnecky.
{ Inversnecky Blues.

R 513 { The Village Editor.
{ The Inversnecky Photographer.

R 514 { The Limb o' the Law.
{ In My Gairden.

R 515 { The Inversnecky Doctor.
{ The Village Grocer.

R 516 { The Story That I Started.
{ Inversnecky Moon.

R 603 { The Weddin' o' Wee MacGregor.
{ Flitting.

HARRY GORDON and
JACK HOLDEN.

R 633 Golf, Two Parts.

R 634 { The Compleat Anglers.
{   Two Parts.

R 635 { Joining the Force.
{   Two Parts.

R 636 { The Piano Tuners.
{   Two Parts.

10 inch Double-sided Records 3/- each

PARLOPHONE RECORDS

Ask your Dealer for Special Scottish Supplements.

8.   Harry, the prolific recording star. This advert dates from August 1930.

9. 'The Gang' - May 1932. The pioneers that Season included Arthur Ackerman and Jenny Wynne; Muriel Farquhar; the Mason Sisters and Dawson Reid.

10. From left to right; Harry; the popular violinist De Groot; and Sir Harry Lauder, all enjoy a chat in the Palace Hotel, Aberdeen. 1934.

5.   BEACH PAVILION   ACT II

The new Aberdeen Beach Pavilion opened on 4th May, 1928, a comfortable, intimate theatre which ideally suited Harry Gordon and his concert party - 'Harry Gordon and his Entertainers'- as they were billed. With its limited seating capacity of about 750 it was perfect for Harry's own homely and chatty style and he talked and joked with his audiences, establishing an unequalled rapport with them long before the modern concept of audience participation.

Harry gave his Aberdeen admirers a foretaste of his Beach Pavilion summer seasons with the snappy revues 'Inversnecky Calling' and 'Inversnecky Snips' in March 1932, 1933 and 1934 at the Tivoli (Theatre of Varieties) in Guild Street. 'The Press and Journal' reported on his first engagement - 'Fresh from his Glasgow pantomime success, Harry was at the top of his form in fun and frolic in a well balanced programme. As he might express it himself he daun'ered through most of the show. His two main turns 'The Explorer' and 'The Student' were great hits. His quips and gags bore the hall-mark of originality. Jack Holden gave his splendid support in several burlesques, notable among which was 'The Hiker'.'

At the Beach Pavilion Harry Gordon could usually rely on the loyal support of Aberdeen friends and visitors. In 1931, for instance, about 400 season ticket holders had seats reserved for the second house on a Saturday.

One of the most daring steps taken by Harry Gordon and his partner Cissy Murray was their decision to bring an internationally known star performer into the show. This bold move occasioned them much thought before arriving at a decision because of the financial risk involved. The regular concert party was already made up of artists who commanded good salaries, while overheads were large - it was therefore a considerable gamble to book an artist at a three-figure fee on top of an already expensive bill. However, they decided to go ahead with the venture, which happily turned out to be a success, in that it not only added to the Pavilion's local popularity but also to its high reputation much further afield 'the acme of concert party perfection' - as one critic remarked.

The first of these special guest artists to be engaged was De Groot, the famous violinist who appeared in June 1929. He was accompanied by David Bor (piano) and H.M. Calve (cello) who later adopted the stage name Don Rico. De Groot brought to the Beach Pavilion many 'highbrows' who had never before been inside the building. At one matinee performance there was an elderly lady who had professedly come to hear De Groot and nobody else. Halfway through the programme when the great violinist still had not made his appearance she grew impatient: leaving her seat she made for the entrance, where she asked the commissionaire, "How much longer have I to stand this tripe? When does De Groot come on?". De Groot was most enthusiastic about the reception he received, and not only did he play for half an hour on his own, but he took up a position in the wings and played little obligatos to the songs as they were sung.

The famous Russian vocal ensemble, the Bayan singers, captivated everyone by the beautiful rendering of their native folk-songs. The Bayan singers had a fortnight's engagement and during the first week Harry Gordon persuaded them to put into rehearsal 'Annie Laurie' and the following week they sang their own arrangement of this in a manner which would have done credit to any native-born group. One of the oustanding guest solo singers was Jose Collins. She had been the little dancer in Sir Harry Lauder's presentation of 'I love a lassie' and had gone on to be the star of H. Fraser-Simpson's musical comedy 'The Maid of the Mountains'. Jose was a rather temperamental artist but fortunately she accepted very readily the limitations of the Beach Pavilion as regards its single stage setting, and a solo piano providing the accompaniment. In fact during her stay Jose Collins became very friendly with Harry Gordon's daughter, and offered to remain another week and work for nothing, a magnanimous offer of which Harry was unable to take advantage since contracts had already been made for that week.

One of the highest paid artists ever to appear on the Beach Pavilion stage was Jack Smith, the world-famous 'Whispering Baritone'. His style was all the rage thanks to the success of his gramophone records which greatly attracted Harry Gordon. He became a 'Jack Smith' enthusiast, carrying his records about with him along with his portable gramophone, and needing little excuse to produce them and give an impromptu recital to the stage hands in the various halls he was then visiting. Although it seemed a forlorn hope at the time, Harry expressed the wish that he could bring the great Jack Smith to the Pavilion. Eventually, however, it did come about that Harry was able to offer him an engagement for a week in August 1930 - an offer which was accepted and despite his large fee, the venture proved a financial success.

Jack Smith who was very happy at the Pavilion, being particularly intrigued with the sketches in the Scots dialect. During that week Harry Gordon and Jack Holden were featuring in a fishing scene in which the running gag was 'Wha' a fush! Wha' a fush!! Wha' a fush!!!'. Jack Smith was in the wings every time this sketch was put on, and nobody laughed more heartily than he, though some of it had to be interpreted for his benefit. When he got back to America after an extensive tour of the continent, Jack Smith sent a letter addressed to 'Wha' a fush Gordon, Inversnecky, Scotland'.

In it he paid Aberdeen a great compliment. Of all the places he had visited, he wrote, the warmest spot in his heart was reserved for Aberdeen where he had been so happy.

Others who appeared at the Beach Pavilion were The Western Brothers - 'the cads with the old school ties', Arthur Cox - who became a leading operatic star, Mona Gray - well-known mimic, Leslie Sarony - the well-known song writer and comedian famous for his song 'Don't do that to the poor Puss Cat', Anona Winn, the popular radio star, Bratza - the Serbian violinist, Billy Mayerl - 'The master of syncopation', Bud Flanagan and Chesney Allen, Birrell O'Malley - who went on to achieve fame as Don Carlos, the radio tenor, Ann Penn - another star mimic, Bennett and Williams - well-known broadcasting artists with their phono-fiddles, Robert Naylor and Sylvia Cecil - famous vocal duo, Flotsam and Jetsam, Vanessa Lee (when she still used the name Ruby Moule, before Ivor Novello rechristened her) and Webster Booth, the well-known Gilbert and Sullivan tenor.

It would appear too that these artists enjoyed their visits to the Beach Pavilion. Many joined in the family party atmosphere which permeated the shows and which also extended backstage. On matinee afternoons, the whole cast would meet for tea in the largest dressing room where a long table was set up and everybody would sit round with Harry Gordon presiding at the top - rather in the manner of J. B. Priestley's 'Good Companions'.

Harry Gordon found time to publish in 1931, a book of 'Inversnecky Yarns'. The following is characteristic:

SUCH IS LIFE

Things were dull in Inversnecky and it was a dull morning too. Andra Benzie called at a neighbour's house. He was met at the door by his friend's wife, and the conversation which ensured went thus -

'Cauld?'

'Aye.'

'Gaun tae be wet, I'm thinkin'.'

'Aye.'

'Is John in?'

Oh aye! He's in.'

35

'Can Ah see 'im?'

'Na.'

'Bit Ah winted tae see 'im.'

'Aye, bit ye canna see 'im. John's deid.'

'Deid?'

'Aye.'

'Sudden?'

'Aye.'

'Verra sudden?'

'Aye, verra sudden.'

'Did he say onything aboot a pottie o' green pent afore he dee't?'

In addition to these famous names, there were the old favourites around whom the programmes were built, principal amongst them Jack Holden and Alice Stephenson. Harry Gordon and Jack Holden's comic duo repertoire quickly grew including such favourites as 'Hiking', 'On a Pillion', 'A Permanent Wave', 'Joining the Forces', 'The Complete Anglers', their double act spot being one of the highlights of the programme.

Alice Stephenson, sister of Cissy Murray, continued as pianist - she was not only a most versatile and accomplished accompanist but she enhanced the stage with her striking appearance.

One new feature which Harry had introduced to the old Pavilion and which continued when the new building opened was a chorus of dancing girls to form a background to the musical numbers. The first group of dancers were the Three Gordon girls, later to be replaced by the Four Tiller Girls. Outstanding local performers were also given their chance at the Beach Pavilion, the singers Margaret Middleton, Margaret Milne and Ronald Robb as well as the Miller Brothers, William on the violin and Jimmy on the piano, who went on to form the Squadronaires and subsequently succeeded Carroll Gibbons at the Savoy Hotel, London. One regular feature at the Beach Pavilion were 'Crazy Nights' - deriving from De Haven and Page where all the performers played anyone but themselves - and eveybody seemed to enter into the spirit of things. The unexpected was however often likely to happen. Visiting artists appearing at the other theatres in the town often used to drop into the Saturday matinee audience at the Pavilion. One week Naughton and Gold of the Crazy Gang were appearing at the Tivoli and duly paid a visit to the Pavilion, sitting in the front stalls where they were spotted by Harry who lost no time in exploiting the situation. First he announced to the mystified audience that there was someone out front of whom he did not approve and whom he did not think they should allow to remain. Two attendants then snatched up Gold and frog-marched him down the aisle and out the side door, before he had time to resist.

The most important ingredient in the success of the concert party at the Beach Pavilion was Harry Gordon himself both as performer and entrepreneur, acting as catalyst and father figure keeping, it seems, everybody happy. In the 1930's, Harry took over as sole lessee of the Pavilion. Important members of staff who helped him in its continued success were J. C. Parkinson - business manager, who also went with him on tour; Chas. Gordon, his brother - stage manager; and James Grieve - electrician. It would have to be something quite catastrophic to bring down the final curtain.

Despite the onset of hostilities the 1940 Beach Pavilion season opened as usual in May. Harry had been associated with the theatre continuously since 1913, with breaks only during the First World War and in 1923 and since he became lessee in 1924 had built up a tremendous reputation for 'Harry Gordon and his Entertainers'. However, despite the Aberdeen public's loyalty to Harry, the blackout and the threat of German air raids deterred people from venturing down to the beach. The only protection offered to patrons was a solitary machine gun situated on the promenade opposite the Beach Pavilion's front door. So, with no audiences to speak of, the 1940 Beach Pavilion season came to an abrupt end on July 6th, and a unique epoch in Scottish entertainment was at an end.

On 29th July, Harry went into a new edition of 'Gaiety Whirl' at the Ayr Gaiety, supported by Jack Holden, while the tenor Walter Midgley was also in the cast. It was a curious thirteen week season, with the Gaiety feeling the pinch of restrictions which affected nearly all aspects of life in Britain. The resident cast had to fill the bill by themselves as several attempts to book guest artists were unsuccessful. Nevertheless for Harry Gordon there was something of the atmosphere of the Aberdeen Beach Pavilion. The Ayr Gaiety was a family theatre run at this time by Eric and Leslie Popplewell, sons of the enterprising Ben Popplewell whose name was synonymous with good family entertainment. This was Harry Gordon's sole run in a 'Gaiety Whirl'.

The next significant step was when Harry joined 'Half-Past Eight' in 1943 and he was associated with editions of that show and 'Five-Past Eight', as it later became, for the remainder of his life.

What of the Aberdeen Beach Pavilion? After the Second World War, Harry Gordon did not renew his lease. The increase in rent required by Town Council coupled with all the other increases in management costs indicated to him that to run a summer season with the calibre of artists employed in pre-war days was no longer an economic proposition. Many still regard it as a source of regret that Harry was 'priced out' of the theatre which he had made famous, but he had the good sense to realise that the days of the small intimate Scottish variety threatre were numbered. So there was no lowering of standards, and the abiding memory of the Beach Pavilion is the halcyon days in the 1920's and 1930's when 'Harry Gordon and his Entertainers' was the outstanding feature of the Aberdeen summer holiday season.

Variety shows were not however totally abandoned at the Pavilion. Several promoters attempted to run summer variety shows on pre-war lines, among them A. Ernest Buchan, an Aberdeen sound consultant and Donald Brothers of the Aberdeen cinema family.

During the latters' summer season, George Blackmore, the organist at the threatre organs of the Capitol and Astoria cinemas accompanied at the Hammond electronic organ; he was later to become chief demonstrator for the Hammond Organ Company. Another unsuccessful entrepreneur was Archie McCulloch, who later admitted that he had not heeded Harry Gordon's advice about the economic viability of post-war variety at the Beach Pavilion, and had suffered in consequence.

Eventually the Pavilion's only function was to accommodate children's entertainment on rainy afternoons. As a result the Corporation realised in 1962 that the halcyon days were forever gone and the building subsequently became the licensed Gaiety, a combination of restaurant and pub. In the 1970's however, a change of ownership resulted in something of an upturn in the fortunes of the erstwhile Pavilion, when the Gaiety became Jay-Jay's - featuring 'Caberet, wining, dining and dancing;. Thus despite a new name and a changed appearance live entertainment returned to the Beach Pavilion and the final chapter in its show business history remains to be written.

6. WIFIES AND PANTOMIME

It was perhaps with his 'dame' characterisations that Harry Gordon made his most distinctive contribution to the variety stage and one writer has suggested that it was 'when portraying 'wifies' from places like the Aberdeen Green that the Laird reached the peak of his comic genius'. It seemed too that this was what he enjoyed doing most, for when someone once asked him what characters he enjoyed playing best, he replied, 'I think it's wifies'. Harry could play the 'grande dame', the couthy country woman or the wifie 'having a crack at the stair-head' - roles which endeared him to more than one generation of theatre goers.

Many of these delightful character studies date from the Beach Pavilion era. As 'Eppie, the Auld Fish Wife' Gordon gave a beautifully restrained portrayal of the traditional Aberdeen fish wife selling her wares at the Friday market in the Green. The patter contains references to two of Gordon's famous catch phrases 's'cold today', spoken in snappy North-East accent and 'a awful day of midgies'.

'As I say sayin' - it's a sair fecht tryin' to mak' a livin' nooadays an' it's harder job tryin' to sell fish, especially when they're a fortnicht aul'. Sometimes I have to rise and tak' a walk roon' just to get a breath o' fresh air. You know, I didna think fish hae a sense o' smell at a', d' you?. If they hid, they wouldna smell the way the do. But I have some funny customers though. I mind the other morning, a wifie bocht a bittie o' ling and efter dinner time she brought it back again and said, 'Eppie, this ling is no a bit like the piece I got a fortnight ago', and I said, 'Well, it should be, it's the same fish'.

And another wifie came up to me and said 'That's a fine piece of cod' and I said 'Excuse me, madam, that's not cod - it's hake', and she said 'It's the price I'm referring to'. Aye, you've to watch them - some o' them are awfy cheeky things - the customers, I mean. A laddie came up to me the other day and he had the impudence to ask me if I was givin' coupons awa' wi' my smokies.

You know I'm awfy bothered with palpitations, so I always keep a bottlie o' - eh - throat salve under this boxie here - and one day I was ha'in a tottlie when a minister came by and he said, 'Oh my good women, shame on you. I am sixty years of age and have never yet tasted liquor' so I said, 'Well, well dinna fash yersel', you're nae going to start now', and he said 'Is this the only consolation you have left in this world, and I said ' No, I've another bottlie under here'.

And 'What's that, missus - oh, a bunchie o' yellows certainly - eh - oh, a codlin, oh, there's a nice fresh one just in this morning. That'll be nine pence please. Yes. Been

39

an awfully cold day today - hasn't it - been an awful day of midgies too - aye - oh, well well we'll send it with the van - just leave the name and address with the typist - thank you very much - thanks. What's that? If you dinna like it, you'll send it back. Oh you dinna need to dae that; just give the fish its instructions and it'll come back itsel'!

A vivid depiction of the backstreet virago comes through in 'The Ghost o' Mistress McIntyre', one of Archie Hyslop's most characteristic songs, full of clever local allusions - which is complemented by its forceful tune in the minor mode.

THE GHOST O' MISTRESS McINTYRE

1. Has onybody seen the ghost o' Hanry McIntyre?
   I've socht him in the ceety an' I've socht him in the shire
   I've wandered inta every public hoose that I've come till.
   In life he used to haunt them an' I bet he haunts them still.
   We focht without cessation frae oor very weddin' day
   Till he shuffled off this mortal coil, which marked the close o' play:
   An' though I followed oot o' spite as fast as I could get,
   For once he'd got a start o' me, an' I hivna catched him yet.

   > CHORUS: I'm the ghost o' puir aul' Mistress McIntyre,
   > Late o' Little Belmont Street,
   > Oh Help me if you can
   > I've haunted Hades, Heeven an' the Castlegate,
   > Wheechin' through eternity,
   > Looking' for my man.

2. For the look o' things I tried aloft, though Henry wisna sharp -
   He couldna play the ukelele, left aleen the harp
   The gentleman on duty said, 'For whom div you inquire?'
   I said 'Hiv you a lodger o' the name o' McIntyre?'
   'McIntyre?' says he, an' passed his hand across his broo,
   'I'm awfu' sorry, mum, we're kin o' oot o' Macs the noo'.
   I said I cam frae Aberdeen his face began to freeze.
   Says he, 'For folk frae Aiberdeen, the ither department please'.

3. An' whit an awfu' crood there wis when I got doon the stair.
   It minded me on Union Street the week o' the Glesga fair.
   An polismen in 'tails wis busy keepin' fowk at bay,

An' Auld Nick's face wis red wi' shoutin' Early doors this way.
'Hiv you a Henry McIntyre?' I askit when fornenst him
He tried to freeze me in a look, but the climate was against him,
'I canna move for Macs', he answered, much to my amazement,
'An if he comes frae Aiberdeen, then try the bargain basement'.

4.   I entered. There wish Union Street as plain as plain could be
An a' yon cats on Union Bridge was spittin' fire at me,
The streets wiv paved in reed-hot brimstane caseys frae the Quarry,
Doon Market Street a line o' buses ran to Purga - Torry,
Along Auld Nicholas Street a tram went by wi' jolts an' slams.
An' I kent then whhit had happened to the auld Surbaban trams.
An' mony a weel-known face I say - aye lots o' them were swells,
But fit's the eese o' telling ye? Ye'll see them for yersels.

5.   But Henry wisna in so quickly back to earth I came,
To see if he wis hauntin' oor or someone else's hame,
I stepped into the wash-hoose an' met blin' aul Mrs. Grubb,
An' she thocht I was a white thing, so she put me in the tub.
The wringer wis the next step an attention I forestalled
By slippin' doon below again wi' an awfu' dose o' cauld
An' there I shook an' sneezed an' shivered, much to Auld Nick's ire.
Says he, 'Hey, stop yer snevvelin' ye're pittin' oot the fire'.

6.   So that is why I haunt the earth as lonely as can be,
An' no one but Sir Oliver Hodge is interested in me.
An' when I'm feelin' cauld an chilled, with neither bite nor sup,
I listen in tae Hazlehead, an' that aye warms me up.
An' when the weather's fine a dander oot by Cults I tak'
An' gie the Shakkin' Brig a fricht - it's me that make it shak,
I've niver met my Henry yet - perhaps a good thing too.
He never saw through me in life, but he'd fair see through me noo.

A song such as 'The Ghost o' Mistress McIntyre' requires impeccable diction, which was of course Harry Gordon's forte. Some of the words of this were adapted by Archie Hyslop, and the song with a different tune became 'Where is my wandering Boy', the hit of the 1930 Edinburgh pantomime 'Mother Goose'. The following is a comparison verse from 'Where is my wandering boy'.

And then they took me doon below and what a crowd was there.

Auld Nick was very busily employed in his abode
Directing a' the traffic at the end o' the Lothian Road
And then a tramway car went past wi' many jolts and jars,
And I knew then what had happened to the gold old cable cars,
And lots o' Edinburgh folk looked pleased as they went passed,
You see there is no East wind there so they were warm at last.

The last line of the chorus was 'He has left me in a hurry for the lichts o' Edinburry'. Inevitably Harry's great ability to introduce topical references came into play when singing the song in Aberdeen. On 28th February, 1931, tramcar services were abandoned on the Torry route, so that summer at the Beach Pavilion the last line became 'He has left me in a hurry on the last tram to Torry'. 'Where is my wandering boy' had a good singable chorus and it was one of those popular audience participation numbers, but the native Aberdonian will still relish the satirical bite of 'The Ghost o' Mistress McIntyre'.

In several of the comic duos with Jack Holden, Harry plays the female part. More rarely as in 'The Washing Day' they are both wifies - 'Rub-a-dub-dub, twa wives at the tub', exchanging wash-house gossip - a now unknown phenomenon in the days of twin-tubs and tumble driers.

As boy and girl in one of their best known sketches 'Hiking', a little sentimental flirtation is allowed to occur before things are brought firmly to earth.

Holden	'You know it's beginning to get dark now and - eh, Teenie, Ah want to speak to you.
Gordon	'Do you?'
Holden	'Look at the coos in the field - they're still rubbin' noses. You know, Teenie, we've been hikin' together every Sunday for the past six weeks, haven't we? And Ah've taken you to the pictures every Wednesday haven't I Teenie?'
Gordon	'Yes'
Holden	'Are you not beginning to smell a rat? Teenie?'
Gordon	'Yoo-hoo.'
Holden	'See the coos?'
Gordon	'Yes.'

Holden	'You know, Ah would like to rub noses too.'
Gordon	'Would you, John.'
Holden	'Yes Ah'd like to rub noses.'
Gordon	'Well come on then.'
Holden	'Well come on then.'
Gordon	'Come on then.'
Holden	'Come on then.'
Gordon	'I'll haud the coo.'

Of course a literal transcription cannot convey the marvellous rapport and ability to play up to each other which existed between Harry Gordon and Jack Holden. Timing was the essence of their success and the simplest material became transformed by their skilful delivery.

As 'Mistress Gordon frae Aiberdeen' and 'Mistress Holden from Kirkcaldy', Harry and Jack captured with venomous accuracy sharp tongue interchange between wifies.

| Holden | 'Well I'd rather be a Fifer than a Aiberdonian any day. I was born in Fife and brocht up in Fife and I hope to live all my life and to dee in Fife.' |
| Gordon | 'Good gracious, woman, have ye nae ambition?' |

Harry was particularly funny playing the wifie speaking in an exaggeratedly genteel manner who would unexpectedly come out with a down to earth vernacular turn of phrase belying her 'refinement'. He used to play a ballroom sketch in which he danced a fox-trot with Jack Holden. After such observations as 'lovely band' and 'magnificent company' came the comment 'but isn't the fleer afful skitey?'

Harry Gordon in the Inversnecky days at the Beach Pavilion was perfecting the art of female impersonation, impersonations which led in time to the classic series of dame studies in pantomime at the Glasgow Alhambra. Albert Mackie in his interesting book 'The Scottish Comedians' which is full of personal recollections of the great stars, recalls one of the performances which he found particularly funny.

'Harry was a farm hand discussing the farmer and his wife. This was the theme of many a bothy ballad from the North-East - the class feeling on the farm - but Harry gave it his own individual twist. The farmer had married a former mannequin - or, as Gordon pronounced it 'mannie quyne' (quyne being the common Aberdeen word for a girl). 'Ye should see her feeding the hens!' and here Gordon mimed this operation, using all the simpering gestures, the walk, the twists and turns of a model at a dress show while obviously scattering grain to the chickens. So that despite his excellence in verbal wit, he could vary it with good visual comedy.'

Clem Ashby who succeeded Jack Holden as Harry Gordon's feed, felt that the prime dame study of Harry's was the Glasgow wifie or Aberdeen wifie - or any other Scottish town for that matter - grey hair, straw hat with a hat-pin through it (or sometimes just an ordinary bonnet if she was away to the 'steamie') - an old cloth cap; teeth out; skirt right under the ankles; elastic sided boots; expounding on all the sins of the neighbours and all the imperfections of her man.

In later years Harry was at his best in 'The Opening o' the Kirk Bazaar', as the wifie criticising everybody else - based, of course, on the comedian's own shrewd observations of female behaviour.

> 'Yon Mrs. McAlpine, she was there:
> 'Mind you I am not a bit catty but yon woman! Oh!! I just canna stick
> her - yon kind o' woman you've to look at twice - canna believe it the
> first time. Seventeen stone if she's a day. I have never seen so many
> women in one lump. And you know she's got so many double chins
> you think she's peepin' o'er a plate o' pancakes.'

During the 1920's and 1930's in Aberdeen, Harry Gordon worked a great deal for the B.B.C., in those pioneering days under the inspired direction of Moultrie Kelsall. One of the small number of dedicated contributors who worked from the old studios in Belmont Street was Arthur Black, stalwart actor and brilliant scriptwriter perfectly capturing the bitter tang of North-East humour. Black collaborated with Harry Gordon in several recordings written by the former, such as 'Fish', 'The Dentist's Chair', 'Stung', 'At the Photographers' and 'Mrs. McIntyre visits the sick'.

In the last of these Harry Gordon as Mrs. McIntyre is ostensibly trying to cheer up Johnny played by Arthur Black.

Mrs. McIntyre   I would hardly have kent you. Ae my but yer face is just
                     like a bawbee's worth o' tea aned ye're as thin as a sparra's

wind pipe. Fou are ye keepin' Johnny laddie? Nae very
well I've nae doubt.

Johnny   Not a bit of it - I'm feeling better every day.

Mrs. McIntyre   Now John, dinna build up false hopes, whatever else ye dae.

Johnny   Oh, I wish I was back to work again.

Mrs. McIntyre   Oh can I believe my ain ears - whit wis that ye said?

Johnny   I wish I was back to work again.

Mrs. McIntyre   Oh, just whit I thocht, I knew it could come to that; eh,
                poor man I'm sorry for ye, ye're deleerious. I'm richt
                sorry to see a young man like you struck down in the prime
                o' life but I'm glad I cam in to see ye just to cheer ye up.

This may be fairly described as Aberdeen humour at its most characteristic and the
opportunity of working with Arthur Black added considerably to Harry Gordon's
rich experience in developing his 'wifie' characters.

Harry Gordon was never happier than when in costume for a character part, male or
female, and his flair for this kind of comedy was given scope in his many appearances
in pantomime. Like the English epitome of pantomime drag, Dan Leno, he also
played such male roles as Idle Jack in 'Dick Whittington', but it was in the dame roles
that he achieved real renown. Unlike the creations of contemporary dames as Danny
La Rue, all Harry's studies were strangers to the doubtful or dirty joke. In the present-
day threatre, Stanley Baxter, who worked with Gordon in 'Five Past Eight' in the
1950's still steers a middle course with his pantomime studies. His extravagant
dresses are in the best tradition, while his comedy, not too sophisticated nor too
juvenile, still owes much to older dames of the Scottish variety theatre.

Harry Gordon's first pantomime engagement was at The Pavilion, Glasgow in
'Aladdin'. Harry was engaged to play the part of Abanazar while his wife was given
the role of Pekoe, the second boy. Both worked very hard to justify their engagement
and subsequent events proved that they succeeded. The first pantomime taught
Harry a great deal; the script as written was far too long and drastic pruning had to
occur before the show settled down to its 'two houses a night' format.

In the 1920's, when Harry had joined forces with Hugh Ogilvie, they toured several pantomimes trading under the name Grahame Watson. Going against established tradition in the profession, they called their first pantomime 'Rip Van Winkle'. Despite this break with convention the pantomime toured successfully for 16 weeks, visiting such theatres as the Hippodrome, Hamilton, and the Alhambra, Stirling - where the scenery had to be adapted to suit the varying stage facilities. At the Metropole, Glasgow, Harry, an inveterate practical joker, had played a trick on the stage hands and they, looking round for a means of getting their own back, found a huge property pie a most convenient vehicle. They filled the pie with heavy weights used for keeping down the scenery. In the pantomime there was a picnic scene in which Harry had to carry this pie on to the stage and out of which in due course he drew property sausages and other articles. On this particular night Harry went to lift the pie as usual but was surprised to find that he could not move it. There was no time to investigate, so exerting all his strength, Harry lifted the pie and staggered on to the stage where it was dropped into the midst of an astonished picnic party. The joke was taken in good part but Harry stipulated afterwards that if the stage hands wanted to play jokes on him they must not require him to perform weight-lifting feats. In face of this ban they showed their resourcefulness and a night or two later when Harry opened the pie out jumped a little pekinese dog belonging to Harry's wife. The audience much enjoyed this incident, as much a surprise to the actors as to them. Indeed it was so popular that the business was retained at subsequent performances.

Harry's pantomime tours, which acquired a widespread reputation, continued until 1929, with such favourites as 'Humpty Dumpty', 'Dick Whittington', 'Goody Two Shoes' and 'Mother Goose'. Harry's wife, under her stage name of Jose Goray appeared in all the pantomime tours until she retired from the stage in the late 1920's. She, however, continued to support him professionally with advice on his costumes and other aspects of his dame studies, and in later years Harry, who by then had ascended to the No.1 dressing room in Glasgow or Edinburgh, always hung a photograph of his wife in 'Aladdin' there, not only as a reminder of what an excellent artist she herself had been, but also of what he owed to her in the advancement or his own career.

Touring and adapting the productions to fit the different halls and theatres gave rise to many incidents. In 1928 a new hall was opened at Kilsyth and Harry, Hugh Ogilvie and Jack Holden produced 'Humpty Dumpty' there. The scenery was so big that even the smallest pieces would not get through the biggest doors, and as this startling discovery was made only a fews hours before the performance was due to begin, a hectic and anxious time was experienced before the doors were enlarged to allow the passage of some of the smallest pieces of scenery. The larger pieces had to be left in their truck at the railway station.

In this pantomime there was a comedy 'prop' horse - the part of the hind legs was played by Joe Seal who was also the company's property man. Hugh Ogilvie, Jack Holden and Harry Gordon were playing their comedy scene and the point was reached when the horse was due to make its entrance. At that moment, however, Joe Seal was found to be missing. Something in connection with his duties as property man had taken up his attention.

The man who occupied the front legs of the horse had no alternative but to come on alone, and the audience was treated to the highly amusing spectacle of a two-legged horse trotting round the stage with its tail trailing on the ground. To add to the humour of the scene Hugh Ogilvie playing the dame, made his exit as the back of the horse. On this occasion, he had to be hoisted on to the shoulders of 'front legs'. That unrehearsed little scene, which the artists made the most of, was voted the hit of the pantomime that night. Such incidents in these touring pantos further contributed to Harry's experience and the scene was now set for his greatest pantomime successes.

Hugh Ogilvie was a good pantomime dame and the experience of working with him contributed to the success of Harry Gordon's later dame studies. Ogilvie died in October, 1931.

Harry Gordon played in pantomime on several occasions at the Ayr Gaiety including 'Dick Whittington' and 'Goody Two Shoes' with the droll Gus Stratton and it was Ben Popplewell, the Gaiety's owner who, over the years had an uncanny ability for spotting new talent and promising young comedians who recommended Gordon to the prominent producer Julian Wylie and Ernest Edelsten, the London Agent.

As a result in 1929 Julian Wylie invited Harry Gordon to play the title role in 'The Queen of Hearts' at the King's Theatre, Edinburgh. This fulfilled one of Harry Gordon's early ambitions as along with giving his name to the performances at the Aberdeen Beach Pavilion and topping the bill at His Majesty's Theatre, Aberdeen, one of Harry's goals was to appear in a pantomime season at the King's Edinburgh. His comedy partner was Jack Edge who had a very decided weakness for the dish of tripe. His family at home indulged his weaknesses and whenever a parcel arrived for him at the theatre, his colleagues would make a shrewd guess as to what it contained. They were never left in any doubt in any event for Jack was the soul of generosity and unselfishness. It was quite a common occurrence to see Jack and the principal boy dash off the stage into Jack's dressing room where a meal of tripe or pigs' trotters awaited them.

In inviting Harry Gordon to play the principal comedy part at the King's in the following year, in the pantomime 'Mother Goose', Julian Wylie broke with his usual practice. Up to that time had had never engaged the same comedian for the same theatre two years running. The two engagements at the King's, Edinburgh were not only enjoyable, but also very memorable for Gordon because of the happy nature of the company, which he always felt went a long way towards making a success of a production.

Harry never looked back after his initial success at the King's Edinburgh. In 1931 came 'Dick Whittington' in Glasgow. Fay Compton was the principal boy, and one of the jokes in the pantomime was

Holden to Gordon: 'Are you Fay Compton'
Gordon to Holden: 'No! I'm fae Inversnecky'

In those days the principal boy was the real star of the show as it was a novely to see a pretty woman in tights. Harry himself in that pantomime was Idle Jack, Tom D. Newell the Dame with Jack Holden as Alderman Fitzwarren. The hit song of the pantomime was Harry's 'When the Broom Blooms Bricht on the Bonnie Broomielaw', in which Jack the sailor recounts his amorous adventures with lassies from Glasgow and further afield. The record label gives the author of the song as Garth Navy who turns out to be none other than Archie Hyslop, a further neat example of a play on a place name - Gartnavel is a Glasgow district - which the author and composer so relished:

WHEN THE BROOM BLOOMS BRICHT

1.   Oh I'm a jolly sailor boy, an' when I'm no at sea,
     I'm chasin' all the girls or else the girls are chasin' me.
     I've done a bit o' coortin' from Peru to Polmadie,
         An' I love each lassie just the same.
     But Glesga is the place where I go coortin' wi' a will.
     I've coorted Ballahouston an' I've coortit Maryhill.
     For back in dear old Glesca Jack can always get a Jill.
         Oh Glesca's jist a hame frae hame.

     CHORUS: I love the lassies; I'm going to wed them aw
               When the broom blooms bricht on the bonnie Broomielaw.
               But in the meantime I'll hae to sail awaw
               Till the broom blooms brawly on the bonnie Broomielaw.

2.   I ken a bonnie lassie; she lives oot at Auchenshuggle.
     She canna learn to haud her tongue; it aye goes wiggle-wuggle.

I've tried to pit ma word in, but I've given up the struggle,
    But I love the lassie a' the same.
I ken anither bonny lass, an' she lives oot at Govan.
She is a lady-riveter; her ways are very lovin':
She hugs ye till she cracks your ribs, then gives your face a shove in,
    But I love the lassie a' the same.

CHORUS

3. I ken a bonny lass, an' she lives at Cartyne.
    To tak her tae the greyhound race I thocht wid be divine.
    But the dogs ran off wi a' her cash; an' she ran aff wi' mine.
        But I love the lassie a' the same
    I ken anither bonny lass, an' she lives oot at Yoker.
    Her faither is a fireman, an' her uncle is a stoker.
    An' when I popped the quest-i-on, she answered wi' the poker.
        But I love the lassie a' the same.

CHORUS

4. I used tae ken a Wishaw lass when I was young an' greener
    Altho' she lived amang the screes, you couldna meet a cleaner.
    But I ken she cam' frae Wishaw, for Aw Wishaw'd never seen 'er.
        But I etc.
    I had a lass at Shettleston with whom I used tae squabble.
    An' ilka nicht oor coortin used tae finish in a rabble.
    For she had got a temper that was un McGovernable.
        But I etc.

CHORUS

5. I ken anither bonny lass oot at Pollokshields.
    To nobody in beauty and in charm my lassie yields.
    She's a face like Tommy Lorne and a voice like Gracie Fields.
        But I love ma lassie - 'In the name.'
    I ken anither bonnie lassie oot at Auchentoshan.
    Last Halloween she telt me that I wish her wee galoshan.
    Her heart is pure an' white, but oh her lugs are needin' washin'.
        But she says the climate is to blame.

CHORUS

6.   I ken anither bonny lass; she lives in Kelvinside.
To hear the way she speaks I do believe the lassie's tried
To mak' me think that Glesca's on the Thames an' no' the Clyde.
     But I etc.
I ken anither bonny lass; the Brigton's her address.
An' Jimmie Maxton's written her to wish us baith success.
He's goin' to get his hair cut jist to gie's a new mattress.
     But I love the lassie etc.

CHORUS

7.   I ken a bonnie lassie; aye, an' she comes frae Dundee.
An' every nicht she has a pot o' marmalade tae her tea.
An' when I get my lass a kiss, oh how she sticks to me.
     But I etc.
I ken an awfu' bonny lass, she comes frae Aiberdeen.
She's no sae small nor yet sae tall; she's jist the golden mean.
Last week she borrowed sixpence, an' since then she's not been seen.
     But I love ma sixpence jist the same.

CHORUS

After 'Dick Whittington', Harry Gordon found himself with a regular pantomime engagement in Scotland's capital city. 1932 saw 'Jack and the Beanstalk', another Julian Wylie production at the King's Theatre, but it was the Theatre Royal Edinburgh which was the base for the next four pantomimes, productions which moved on for seasons at the Glasgow Pavilion, in 1933 - 'Red Riding Hood', 1934 'Rip Van Winkle' 1935 'Humpty Dumpty' and finally in 1936 'Babes in the Wood'.

In 1937 another landmark was reached in Harry Gordon's career, when he was invited to be principal comedian in what was without any doubt, Scotland's most highly rated pantomime, Tom Arnold's production at the Glasgow Alhambra. This began the record run of sixteen consecutive pantomimes at the Alhambra. The 1937 pantomime was 'Puss in Boots' but it is perhaps the 1938 production of 'Aladdin' which assumes greater significance, because in it, Harry Gordon played the Dame for the first time since 1930, and thus began the series of famous dame studies. If Aberdeen folk remember Harry Gordon particularly because of his concert party at the Beach Pavilion, Glaswegians remember him through his magnificent dame portrayals.

In 1939 he was Buttons in 'Cinderella' and Albert Mackie, 'Macnib', wrote the following rhyme at the time summing up his reactions to his scintillating wit and kindly humour.

'Twinkle, twinkle, little star;
What a perfrect scream you are!
Though your buttons shine so bright,
Brighter still your wit at night.
Many years now - man and boy -
You have worked to give us joy;
Also as a Dame sedate,
We have seen you scintillate.
Now you're Buttons, pert and cherry -
How could Glasgow e'er grow dreary?'

There was no question about his brilliance in this show of Tom Arnold's as reports confirm. He was extremely funny as the conductor of a 'Symphony Orchestra' - a popular sketch which has been done with varying skill. He worked splendidly in diminutive contrast to Big Bertha Belmore who with Mamie Soutter formed the Ugly Sisters, he also sang 'Run, Rabbit, Run' with Muriel Barron. Muriel Barron, who was an Ivor Novello leading lady in several of his shows, was principal boy in several of the Alhambra pantomimes. Harry also threw in impersonations of Lionel Barrymore and the Western Brothers, as well as an operatic aria. He was both equally successful as an evacuee out to disrupt the peace of the 'Big Hoose' that had taken him in and he and Jack Holden had their customary marvellous piece of front-cloth crosstalk in the old tradition.

'The Sleeping Beauty' followed in 1940. Principal boy was Evelyn Laye and also in the cast was Alec Findlay, one of whose turns was playing a set of miniature bagpipes. Years later in the 1970's when 'Amazing Grace' hit the pop charts, Alec was able to reintroduce the bagpipes into his act and scored a success on Grampian Television playing 'Abide with Me', and with The Royal Clansmen won the television award as the leading showbusiness team.

Alec Finlay, if perhaps not the most inspired of Scots comics, was a great showman whose appropriate presentation made the most of his material. Alec Finlay in this pantomime - 'Rudolf the Page' - was later to co-star with Harry Gordon in the Glasgow Alhambra pantomimes. In the 1940 'Sleeping Beauty' Harry's hit number was 'Le Rossignol qui ne chanta point' 'par Re Elrique' written by Archie Hyslop. With the tune a cross between 'A nightingale sang in Berkeley Square' and 'Kelvin

51

Grove' the song neatly combined musical parody with geographical appositeness. 'The nightingale that never sang in oor George Square' was a tremendous success in Glasgow.

LE ROSSIGNOL QUI NE CHANTA POINT

1.   Frae London on the radio the listeners they regale
      With a song about a London square an' London nightingale,
      But I'm a Glesca chap masel' an' so I dinna care
      An awfu' lot whit happens in a place like Berkeley Square,
      For we have got oor sanctuaries a great sicht nearer hame,
      Aye Glesca has its beauty spots no less deservin' fame
      Still I'll admit no nightingale so far has show a flair
      For bouts o' coloratura work in oor George Square.

2.   In ither Scottish towns the nightingales may do their stuff -
      In Perth and Pittenweem they may be plentiful enough
      I'm thinkin' ony nightingale gey tired o' life wad be
      Reduced tae singin' solos in the centre o' Dundee.
      In Golden Square in Aberdeen where lawyer bodies wait
      No nightingale wad ever chunt for less than six and eight
      And in George Square in Edinbro' no nightingale wad dare -
      But we arena' that particular in oor George Square.

3.   The nightingales frae Ro'esay Bay wi' twitterin' treble soft
      May serenade Sir Walter Scott as he sits up aloft
      The robin roon' the scattered seats in search o' crumbs may ramble
      Retirin' tae digest them upon auld Sir Colin Campbell
      And in the shops ayont the Square the hens are in their prime
      Of course their necks are thrawn so they're past their singin' time,
      Upon the Municipal roofs the happy spyugs may pair -
      But ye don't find courtin' nightingales in oor George Square.

4.   From oot the Chamber windaes whaur the Council congregates
      I've heard Lord Provost Dollan gently cooin' tae his mates.
      While from the woods o' Kelvingrove we've listened, have we not.
      To the measured unselfconscious lay of Walter Elliot.
      An' on a starry nicht into ma throat there comes a lump
      At the pure ethereal tones o' Jimmy Maxton on the stump.
      When Jimy agitates his fist and brandishes his hair,
      Whit price a bloomin' nightingale in oor George Square?

52

5.   Ye maybe think it strange tae find a noticeable dearth
O' nightingales in Glesca, the muist kindly place on earth
But the wee bird has a fault for which it's music can't atone -
It won't combine with other birds it aye works on its own.
This with the Glesca Council chaps its chance cannot assist
They don't approve an attitude so individualist
But onywye o' common spyugs we've plenty an' to spare
So wha's botherin' aboot nightingales in oor George Square?

It seems that at this time all Harry Gordon's activities were making theatrical history, for the 1941 pantomime at the Glasgow Alhambra starred both Harry Gordon and Will Fyffe. It would be perfectly fair to say that excluding Lauder, who was by that time virtually in retirement, Will Fyffe and Harry Gordon were the two principal Scotch comedians. Thus the combination of their talents was likely to produce something quite outstanding and so happily it turned out. This friendly pantomime collaboration in fact lasted six years and was one of great events in Scottish entertainment. In the pantomimes Will Fyffe had of course to introduce some of his famous character studies, while Harry stuck more to the pantomime role. In the 1941 'Dick Whittington', Will Fyffe played Idle Jack while Harry Gordon played the dame, always known as Maggie, a sonsy character who was as full of the milk of human kindness as the 'Stovies' she sang about were full of juicy succulence.

The 1942 pantomime 'Jack and the Beanstalk' introduced a parody of that popular B.B.C. radio programme 'The Brains Trust'. The question master Jack Holden (the Squire) asked 'Why are giants tall?' The trustees were Harry Gordon as Professor Goad, Will Fyffe as Commander Scramble and Peggy Carlisle as Professor Tuxley. In 'Jack and the Beanstalk' was introduced a new number which was to become a great favourite - 'The Land Girl'.

And so I'm noo a botman tae a coo,
I'm one of the Land Girls parading wi' my hand upon the plough
From the crack o' dawn till the sun sets in the sky
I'm milking they kye, cleaning the sty
With a ho-de-ho and a hi-de-hi.

Mind you there's another land girl on the farm here and she thinks she's
it, but she knows noting at all about farming, nothing whatsoever.
First time she saw a haystack she says to me 'Oh fancy it growing in
lumps like that.'

1943 saw 'Red Riding Hood' and The Happy Naafi Cookie' - one of Harry Gordon's best numbers, which regrettably he never recorded, with its description of the passion fruit he concocts in his canteen - half a cold potato with a picture of Dorothy Lamour on it. Other highlights of this pantomime were Robert Wilson's show-stopping rendering of 'Macgregor's Gathering' and Will Fyffe and Harry Gordon in a Scottish glen scene as ancient and deaf man and wife. The tradition continued in the 1944 'Robinson Crusoe' with Harry Gordon as 'One of the oldest hens in the W.R.N.S. One of the oldest tugboats in the fleet'. The small and kittenish Betty Frankiss was a delightful Robinson Crusoe. In 1945 came 'The King and Queen of Hearts', Harry as 'Katie, the Queen of the Clippies' and Will as 'The Wee Tattie Bogle' and 'The Returned Warrior'.

Throughout these pantomimes which established Harry Gordon as the greatest Scottish pantomime dame, the highest levels of fun, spectacle and originality were maintained despite the difficult wartime conditions. And always a source of a smile were the catch-phrases such as 'It's in the bag.' This phrase originated in the golfing sketch at the Beach Pavilion. Every time the golfer (Jack Holden) wanted a new ball or club, Harry as the caddy would say 'It's in the bag', and soon the audience was chorusing it with him.

The partnership with Will Fyffe lasted until the 1946 pantomime 'Babes in the Wood'. The following year was a considerable ordeal for Harry as he had to go on not only without his friend and partner but in the knowledge that Will Fyffe was critcally ill. In fact Will Fyffe died shortly afterwards at his hotel in St. Andrew's. One of Harry Gordon's most treasured possessions was a kilt pin in the form of a sword with the Gordon badge which was inscribed 'Tae Maggie fae Wull' - Harry Gordon's dame part was always 'Maggie', playing opposite Will Fyffe as 'Willie'. Will Fyffe presented the kilt pin to Harry Gordon at the end of the 1945 pantomime.

Between them they built up a pantomime partnership which was not only the talk of Glasgow, but of the whole profession - a combination of two comedians working as one towards and ultimate success which is still remembered as a supreme example of artistry, showmanship and mutual understanding. The other aspect of their secret of success was the brotherly bond which grew steadily between them. This 'mutual admiration society', was of course never flaunted in the open. On the contrary, in public appearances, they invariably castigated and insulted each other to the delight of their audiences. In the 1946 pantomime Fyffe referred to Gordon as 'the woman who had to work all summer at the King's Theatre so that she could raise the fare back to Aberdeen'. To this Gordon retorted that it was 'just as good as keeping a wee pub in St. Andrews'.

In the 1945 pantomime 'The King and Queen of Hearts' Will Fyffe and Harry Gordon had a comedy scene which depicted a working family going on holiday to Dunoon. Will and Harry were man and wife and Jack Holden the 'wee boy'. Lord Inverclyde invited them to do a cabaret at a big function in the Central Hotel, Glasgow and they decided to do this Dunoon sketch and go across to the hotel in dress and make-up. A car had been ordered but did not turn up so they flagged down a taxi. It drew into the kerb, the driver took one look at them, said 'Nut on yer Nellie', and drove off. Further efforts to obtain a taxi also failed, so the trio agreed to walk. They received many curious glances with Will Fyffe ambling along in his workingman costume, Harry Gordon in his Victorian costume with bustle at the back and Jack Holden in short trousers.

Will Fyffe was King Rat for a term of the Grand Order of Water Rats, that exclusive stage society in London, which includes in its membership the biggest names in the profession. Harry Gordon was very proud of the fact that in 1945, when he was privileged to be admitted as a member, it was Will Fyffe who swore him in. Harry and Will had travelled together from Aberdeen and they carried in one wee bag a commodity they guarded very carefully all the way and which they knew would be greatly appreciated by the members at the social hour which was to follow the initiation. Unhappily, en route, two of the bottles were broken, and Harry had great joy in telling the company that 'although King Rat Fyffe was a grand comic he was a gey puir porter'.

Harry Gordon gave the address from the pulpit at Will Fyffe's memorial service. Quite suddenly he stopped - it was no pause for effect - tears were welling from his eyes. Harry's memory was of a man who was a master of his art, a genius at mixing humour with pathos and for whom he had always the greatest respect as an artist and a man.

In his subsequent pantomimes at the Alhambra and Glasgow Theatre Royal Harry starred first with Alec Finlay. Finlay was a very good pantomime star - small and neat and with a rather lugubrious expression and a wide 'little boy lost' look which nicely suited such parts as Buttons and Humpty Dumpty. The 1948 pantomime 'Puss in Boots' produced two popular Harry Gordon numbers 'Tessie the Toast of the Trossachs' and 'Steamie Jeanie', while there was a successful sketch with Alec Finlay as a statue of William Wallace having a chat with Mary Queen of Scots (Harry Gordon). In the 1952 pantomime 'Jack and the Beanstalk', Alec Finlay introduced one of his most effective character studies 'The Auld Kirk Elder'. By this time Harry Gordon's repertoire of female studies was complete. He could switch from 'When I was a Mannequin at Daly's' to Annie Oakley, to studies of a rather grubby schoolgirl

'A bud about to flower into womanhood', or of a very unattractive young woman eating fish and chips. For the 1950, 51 and 52 pantomimes Harry Gordon and Alec Finlay were joined by Duncan Macrae and Robert Wilson to produce an all-star cast, while principal boys included Jill Manners and Joan Stewart. The 1950 'Cinderella' saw an extraordinary trio of female impersonators - Harry Gordon as Gorgeous Gussy, Duncan Macrae as Dame Sybil and Donald Layne-Smith as Marlene. Harry Gordon subsequently collaborated with Jack Radcliffe and Jimmy Logan, and it was remarkable how in the 50's his shows held out against the onset of television, but one of his great features was the constant freshness of his material.

In pantomime, in addition to his verbal brilliance there were his magnificent dresses. Under the direction of Minnie Simpson who had been Florrie Forde's dresser, Harry appeared in one outrageous costume after another, although his costumes over the years gradually became less extravagant and more beautifully tailored. Minnie Simpson ruled the roost in the dressing room with the authority of a true expert. Harry Gordon, as always, invited other members of the cast into his dressing room for morning tea. Minnie Simpson kept a careful watch on the proceedings and would not allow any cup to be removed from the dressing room. On one occasion, things were going wildly wrong at a full production rehearsal and tempers were getting rather frayed. The whole situation was defused when Minnie Simpson glided on to the stage with the words 'I'm looking for a cup'. Under her direction Harry was always impeccably attired. Particularly effective was his costume for 'The Dowager Duchess of Dirleton on the Dirle; here he was an elderly lady of style and elegance, petite, chic, dressed in black with silver wig and parasol. His poise and deportment were exemplary. The Alhambra pantomimes continued to be the top Christmas entertainment and this at a time when other Glasgow theatres were also offering a first class show. There might be Jack Anthony at the Pavilion, Dave Willis at the Theatre Royal as well as the newly introduced 'pantos on ice'. The Alhambra run was broken in 1953 when Harry Gordon starred with Jimmy Logan in 'Puss in Boots;' at the Theatre Royal.

Following his heart attack at the end of 1955 Harry was unable to fulfil his pantomime engagement at the Theatre Royal, Glasgow. His place as dame in 'Dick Whittington' was taken by a young and virtually unknown comedian, Andy Stewart. It would be wrong to suggest that Andy Stewart's forte was playing pantomime dame, but this pantomime helped bring attention to himself and he subsequently became a well-liked Scots singer/comedian in the Lauder tradition.

Many thought Harry Gordon unwise to return to the theatre after his serious heart attack but the comedian's life was so much a part of his make-up that he was unhappy doing anything else and on 24th November, 1956 he opened at the Theatre Royal, Glasgow in 'Robinson Crusoe'. In late December, he was struck down by influenza and he died the following January.

7.   'CURIOUSLY EUPHONIC'

As it transpired, radio and later television were between them to supersede to a great extent the live theatre, and particularly the music hall, as a means of mass entertainment but to Harry Gordon the radio was an important medium. In the 1920's when the Inversnecky period was in full swing, he became an enthusiastic radio artist in considerable contrast to many other managements who regarded the 'wireless' with deep suspicion assuming that their shows would be 'wasted'. Harry Gordon welcomed the B.B.C. and arranged his performances to suit the unseeing audiences. In 1935 the radio critic Rex King wrote 'The first batch of the outside broadcasts from the holiday resorts have arrived. I give them a welcome. Amongst them you are sure to find many pleasant surprises and a few winners. The first was a winner. It was sent over by Harry Gordon, from Aberdeen, and might I, at this early point, draw the attention of the summer concert parties to the finished way Harry sent over the broadcast? I felt this was a complete broadcast specially devised for listeners... What I like about Harry is that his unexpected replies always sound as if they might actually have been spoken by someone in real life. It is the mark of a great comedian. It was the first time I had heard his Dominee character, and the letter from his pupils were all fresh to me'.

In addition to network broadcasts throughout the British Isles, Harry's broadcasts were sometimes heard further afield. In September 1935,he did a midnight broadcast from the Beach Pavilion - the broadcast going directly to South Africa and India and recorded for relay to Canada and Australia.

In November 1939 he made his 100th broadcast. In addition to broadcasts live from the Beach Pavilion, Harry was a frequent visitor to Aberdeen's Radio Station which broadcast as 2BD, at that time in Belmont Street. Harry was as meticulous in the presentation of his broadcasts as he was in his stage shows, as Howard Lockhart later recalled. 'Every word was written down beforehand in his own handwriting, on margined sheets of ruled foolscap that he kept for the purpose. The procedure proved of special value to us when war came and censorship forbade the ad lib or unscripted word'. In addition, Harry was perfect working from a script - in contrast to many comedians who are very successful with memorised material laced with ad libs but are awkward straight readers. Harry Gordon's clean and wholesome comedy was ideal for Children's Hour for which he supplied 'Inversnecky Bairns'.

On October 2nd 1935, the Aberdeen Wireless Station broadcast 'The Trial of Harry Gordon'. This was a travesty based on the series 'Famous Trials' broadcast by the B.B.C. the previous winter. The cast included Harry Gordon, Jack Holden, Phil

Morgan, at that time a favourite guest artist at the Beach Pavilion, and John Foster, one of the broadcasting pioneers in Aberdeen, as the judge. The charge was 'poaching salmon' and at the end when Harry Gordon had been found not guilty by the jury and acquitted, he invited everybody round for their tea - salmon, of course. So successful was this programme that 'The Trial of Harry Gordon' was later broadcast throughout the network.

Two years later came another memorable broadcast - 'Thunder over Inversnecky', broadcast 29th - 30th April 1937 and written by Archie Hyslop. It included Willie Meston playing the 'oldest councillor' Shinnlespanks (a play on the name of his popular radio character Alexander Spinnie Shanks.) In reality this sketch was an elaborate means of introducing various of Gordon's best known numbers such as 'Inversnecky Pub', 'Inversnecky Lasses' and 'Inversnecky Blues'.

Harry's broadcasting career continued unabated until the end of his career. He appeared in 'Worker's Playtime' and his own series of B.B.C. features, including 'Harry's Half Hour', 'Harry's Choice', and 'Gordon Gaieties'. Such artists as Molly Weir and Margo Henderson appeared with Harry in this series. His ability to adapt his act so that it was funny to both live audience and the listening audience was one of his great talents. His popularity as a broadcaster extended to his inclusion along with 'Big Hearted' Arthur Askey and Richard 'Stinker' Murdoch in 'Radio Fun', a popular comic paper launced in 1938. The cartoon series being featured between February and September 1940.

It was just before a broadcast from the Music Hall, Aberdeen in October 1955 that Harry Gordon had his serious heart attack. The producer Iain MacFayden facing one of his first big broadcasts, not only had to get the programme out somehow, but also had to contend with the distraction of the other artists, such as Renee Houston, who were so concered about Harry's condition.

Harry came too early for television to make much use of him but one of his last appearances was in a nationwide televised broadcast of the 'Water Rats', 65th anniversary show when he paid tribute to his old friend Will Fyffe and led the company in 'I belong to Glasgow'. Harry Gordon's last radio broadcast was transmitted on December 22nd, 1956, in a programme to mark the 50th anniversary of both the King's Theatre, Edinburgh and His Majesty's Theatre, Aberdeen.

What made Harry Gordon an ideal radio and gramophone artist was the verbal intensity of his style much more so than comedians such as Tommy Lorne, George West or Dave Willis. Superb diction enabled Gordon to put over his material in a shorter length of time than many of his contemporaries, which made him ideal as a recording artist. The introduction of electric recording, around 1924, had made the gramophone a truly popular and acceptable medium despite the restriction imposed by the record size and the 78 r.p.m. speed.

As with radio, Harry Gordon took to the gramophone as the proverbial fish to water. He was a prolific recording artist. His songs, although necessarily condensed, did not suffer from the transfer to the 10" record side, and his records, made almost entirely between 1926 and the early 1930's are a marvellous legacy of the Inversnecky period. In the early 1930's Harry Gordon was able to write:

> 'I may say that I have recorded perhaps more original songs than any other Scots comedian, having a list of over 135 titles to my name. The making of a gramophone record is a nerve-racking experience. You have no audience to pull you out. You are singing against the clock, for your song must be perfectly timed and there is constantly present the knowledge that you every sound will be faithfully reproduced and that the slightest slip will spoil everything. You are on the stretch all the time'.

Harry Gordon's records at the time of the heyday of the Beach Pavlion and his early pantomime successes in Glasgow and Edinburgh enjoyed immense popularity. At one stage in 1931, they were selling at the rate of 6,000 a week and one title made just before Christmas 1930 sold 22,000 copies within a fortnight of publication.

It should be mentioned that he made some pseudonymous recordings. Edison Bell issued a Harry Lauder selection on four sides by 'Jock MacGregor' with orchestral accompaniment. They were reissued on the 'Mayfair' label, Harry Gordon having now become 'Sandy McPhail'. Jock MacGregor i.e. Harry Gordon also recorded 'Jock's Return on Hogmanay' on Edison Bell, and 'Doon by the Riverside' which Harry sang with much success later in America. Years later, Harry Gordon recalled how he had met Lauder who asked him 'Do you know who this Jack MacGregor is who's been making records of my songs?' Harry, scared to reveal the truth, answered that he had no idea. Lauder replied 'Well if you do meet him, give him my thanks for all the royalties I'm getting'.

Harry Gordon, under his own name made some records on the Actuelle Label (Pathe Freres Pathephone Ltd) of his earlier style songs with Alice Stephenson identified as accompanist. The bulk of Harry Gordon's recorded output however exists on the Beltona and Parlophone labels. Gordon was apparently not contractually obliged to either company and many numbers appear on records of both companies in slightly differing versions.

Harry Gordon made many comedy duo recordings. Some were written by and performed with Arthur Black, one of the stalwarts of the Aberdeen Radio Station. As the Bon-Accord Entertainers - not named on the record label - but in reality Harry Gordon and Arthur Black, they made a 2-sided Beltona 'A mither aye kens' a sentimental sketch in contrast to their usual humorous recordings.

Harry usually played one of his 'wifies' generally 'takin' a len' of the dour Arthur Black - a nice comic contrast. Their sketches included 'Stung', 'The Dentist's Chair' and 'Fish'. In the last of these Arthur Black is the shopkeeper, Harry Gordon the customer.

Gordon: I say George, fit's that ticket in yer window for?

Black: 'Fresh fish sold here'. You surely ken fit that's for.

Gordon: No, no I've nae idea.

Black:'   Fresh fish sold here'. That's to let folk understand that I sell fish.

Gordon: Mercy me. Abody understands that weel enough. You could smell your fish a mile awa.

The Arthur Black, Harry Gordon duos appear on 10" Beltonas.

Also on Beltona are some duos by Harry Gordon and Donald Hunter who was possibly Jack Holden while the bulk of the comedy duo records are by Harry Gordon and Jack Holden under his own name. These appear on both 10" Beltonas (with the smaller blue label and the slightly extended playing time) and 10" Parlophone issues and are versions of their popular stage duos extending over both sides.

It is perhaps the remarkable collection of his comic songs which makes the most facsinating part of Harry Gordon's recorded repertoire. Some of the recordings were immensely popular particularly in Aberdeen and the North-East. The 'best seller' seems to have been 'The Bells of Invernecky', one of Archie Hyslop's best numbers coupled with Harry Gordon's famous 'Inversnecky Fireman'. This was so popular that 'The Bells of Inversnecky' was remade by Beltona backed by another successful Hazelwood number 'The Inversnecky Billposter'.

Closely following 'The Bells of Inversnecky' in recorded popularlity were 'Hilly's

Man', one of Harry Gordon's own numbers.

Another very successful number was 'Fine Man John' (Forbes Hazlewood). Both 'Hilly's Man' and 'Fine Man John' were recorded twice on Beltona, the remake being the only 12" Harry Gordon record issued.

'The Rodin Tree' with its gentle piano accompaniment is also particularly appealing.

THE RODIN TREE

1.   Auld Airchie he sat by the side o' the brook,
Wi' a rod in his hand and a worm on the hook
'Neath the boughs o' a rodin tree shady.
The sunshine cam' lazily fricklin' through:
Aroon' him the flooers sae dinaty o' hue:
They were yalla an' purple an' violet an' blue -
Wi' a hi timmer ha timmer hey-dee.

2.   Auld Airchie caught nothing I'm sorry to say,
Though he sat there and fished through the hale o' the day
'Neath the boughs o' a rodin tree shady:
For into the burnie though he never knew
Cam' the waste fae the gasworks, sae dainty o' hue:
It was yalla an' purple an' violet an' blue -
Wi' a hi timmer ha timmer he dee.

3.   So anither attempt he determined to mak'
But doon on a wasps' nest he set by mistak'
'Neath the boughs o' a rodin tree shady;
An' he got several bites - o' the wrang kind it's true -
An' the language that Airchie let oot when he knew:
It was yella an' purple an' violet an' blue -
Wi' a hi timmer ha timmer hey-dee.

The bulk of the Beltona recordings have one song per side although some extend over both. An interesting example is 'Where is my Wandering Boy today', where the song's pantomime origins are clearly shown in the way Gordon teaches the audience the chorus and gets them to join in. Others include the 'Call o' the Hielans' and 'The Railway Fireman' (The man that maks the smoke come oot the lum). One can sense how Harry had only to sing 'Chug-gy chug, puff-puff, oo-ta-ta' to have Aberdeen audiences in the palm of his hand.

The majority of the Beltona records were made with orchestral accompaniment but one of two are with piano, including the popular 'The Rodin Tree'. On some records, including a late issue comprising 'The Pool at Aberdeen' and 'In the Simmertime', the pianist is named as Alice Stephenson, Harry Gordon's Beach Pavilion accompanist.

Harry Gordon's Parlophone recordings provide interesting comparative recordings of songs such as 'The Auldest Aiberdonian', 'The Story that I startit at the Kirk Soiree' as well as providing the only version of songs such as 'The Dyspeptic' (I'm bad etc.) and 'Inversnecky Blues'.

Parlophone also issued several comic duos with Harry Gordon and Jack Holden. Thus between the two labels many of the popular sketches such as 'Golf', 'Joining the Force', 'The Complete Anglers', 'The Piano Tuners'can still be heard.

After the recession which hit the recording industry as fiercely as any in the mid 1930's, Harry Gordon did not make any more records until he recorded some titles including his Glasgow Alhambra pantomime numbers 'The Land Girl' and 'The Dowager Duchess' in the 1940's for Beltona which had then become part of Decca.

Although there was talk in the 1950's of recording new numbers such as 'Strolling along the Sunny Side of Princes Street', this came to nothing. Fortunately, however, the majority of Harry Gordon's greatest songs are preserved in the remarkable Beltona and Parlphone series. Most of these are remarkably good recordings and it is indeed fortunate that, in contrast to so many other Scots comedians, so much of Gordon's material is so well preserved for posterity.

8.   ENTR'ACTES OUT OF SCOTLAND

In the course of his career, Harry Gordon established a consistent pattern in his professional activities. In the days before the Second World War, these revolved round the summer Beach Pavilion seasons and the Christmas pantomimes. After the war, 'Half-Past Eight' and pantomime were the focal points of his year. In addition to these fixtures in his diary, Harry Gordon took part in many Scottish concert tours, taking in many of the smaller towns which has no proper theatre or could not support the full scale show. There are however many instances of departures from his normal established routine which added variety and touches of extra colour to his career.

One of the earliest of these was Harry Gordon's visit to the London Palladium. It was only to be expected that one of Harry's ambitions like that of many an up and coming artist was to appear on the London stage and it was an ambition which was realised in October 1929. It was an indication of his immense popularity in Aberdeen and the North East of Scotland that a trainload of over 300 Aberdonians travelled on a specially chartered train dubbed the 'Inversnecky Express', to London to cheer on their favourite at his Palladium debut. Londoners on their way to work were startled as the 'Inversnecky Express' steamed into London. Bagpipes skirled, men shouted and cheered, and tartan streamers were flaunted everywhere.

'I'm telephoning my mither tonight - if I'm a success' said Harry. 'If I'm a flop, I'll write.' 'You may be extravagant for once' shouted an Aberdonian. 'Pit in the call right away. We'll show London you're not the Cock o' the North for nothing.' And show London the Aberdonians tried to do - as Harry's familiar dapper figure ambled on to the Palladium stage, the visitors from the 'Inversnecky Express' gave him such a reception that the orchestra was completely drowned out. The conductor had to turn round to request the Aberdonians to 'make a noise a little more quietly.'

Despite this, Harry Gordon was not a conspicuous success in London, although he did make several return appearances there. Indeed the vociferous Aberdonians may have contributed to his comparative failure by antagonizing the more sophisticated London audience, but the real reason for his lack of success is more difficult to ascertain. It was not that his material could not transplant - this could hardly have been the case when his broadcast shows achieved network coverage and were successfully relayed throughout the British Isles and Empire. A possible explanation however does suggest itself. Gordon was not a Scotch comedian of the Lauder style - he was not an exponent of 'kilt with red nose and tammy'. His humour, much more verbal and less obviously Scottish, was different to what London audiences expected from a comedian from North of the Border. Harry Gordon had been, therefore, to all intents and purposes and certainly by his own standards, a 'failure' in England. He wisely decided that for the most part his future should lie in Scotland, a decision which earned him immortality in the history of Scottish variety. Even as late as 1949 he was to comment ruefully, 'South of the Border, some of our native Scots stories fall flat, not on acount of the dialect, but because of the pithiness, paukiness and subtlety which usually forms the ingredients of the Scots joke'.

In 1934 Harry Gordon made theatrical history by giving a performance in Inverness between two houses at the Beach Pavilion at both of which he appeared. Gordon had appeared at the first Beach Pavilion house and left the stage at 7.20. Fifteen minutes later he took off from Seaton Aerodrome in the aircraft 'Aberdeen' belonging to Highland Airways Ltd. and piloted by J. Rae. At Inverness, he was met by Baillie Hugh Mackenzie, Councilor A. A. Noble and Robert Donald of Highland Airways. The party travelled to the natural amphitheatre at the Ness Islands where the performance was to be given. An audience of over 4,000 gave Harry Gordon an enthusiastic reception. At 9.15 p.m. the 'Aberdeen' was back in the air and at 10.15 p.m. it touched down at Seaton and ten minutes later he was back at the Beach Pavilion singing 'The lassie that I love so well' to a packed house.

Several jaunts of this nature took place. In 1935 the Beach Pavilion company flew to Thurso, provided a two hour show there in aid of the Duke of York's Playing Fields Scheme, returning to Aberdeen in time for the first house at the Beach Pavilion. In 1938, the Pavilion concert party gave performances at the famous Empire Exhibition, Glasgow on Empire Day - Tuesday, 24th May. Archie Hyslop wrote a new song for Harry Gordon for the occasion.

Harry was extremely busy on his native soil throughout the 1930's and the hostilities of the Second World War precluded the possibility of any overseas work. He played his part for E.N.S.A. appearing with artists such as the tenor, Robert Wilson and Kathie Kay who achieved subsequent fame with Billy Cotton and his Band. Harry entertained the forces in theatres such as the Marigny on the Champs Elyssy in Paris. Audiences often comprised a substantial proportion of American G.I.'s.

Following the war a further chapter in Gordon's career opened when he began to make concert tours abroad. Harry had in fact been invited to appear in America as early as 1930. During the summer season at the Beach Pavilion that year, one of the guests had been the 'whispering baritone', Jack Smith. Jack had brought his manager Mr. Kemp with him to Aberdeen. Kemp was a most attentive listener to Harry's songs and patter and five weeks later Harry received a telephone message from him just as the performance was about to begin. Speaking from London, he asked Harry if he would come to New York and play in Earl Carroll's Varieties for a year. Harry was astounded both by the invitation and the salary offered but his pantomime and Pavilion engagements made him say a reluctant 'No' to the prospect of playing in New York. The opportunity to go to America did not present itself again until 1947 when he made his first transatlantic concert tour. This was to be the first of several highly successful overseas visits to the United States, Canada, South Africa and Rhodesia. Harry was of course delighted to be following in the footsteps of Sir Harry Lauder, who had achieved an international reputation through his tours of the North American continent.

One of the additional pleasures of these visits was the meeting of many exiles from Scotland. Several of these were Aberdonians who had known Harry much earlier in his career. As always Harry received and entertained these Scots exiles far beyond the call of professional necessity. He met an old Sunday School teacher from Gilcomston Church, an exile from Glasgow who had last seen him in Monty's Pierrots at Stonehaven in 1912 and Alec Kellas from Lumsden in Aberdeenshire. Mr. Kellas had come to Vancouver when the city was in its infancy - a mere collection of shacks and wooden planks for pavements - and had never been home since. However, he still spoke as broad a Doric as any Buchan farmer. As Harry recorded, 'His accent was music to my ears and hig lugs were dirlin' too as I answered him in the same dialect and we both agreed it was gran' growin' wither'. On one trip, Harry was telephoned by someone who introduced himself 'Guess you don't remember me, but I once wrote a song for you, 'Jean from Aberdeen' - remember?' 'Oh aye', Harry replied, vaguely recalling an old number, 'but what's your name again.' 'Oh', said the voice, 'I'm Harry Armstrong. I'm the guy who also wrote a couple of other little songs 'Sweet Adeline' and 'Nellie Dean'. And it was.

Harry had tremendous nostaligic appeal for these expatriates. He used to say 'I went there to make them laugh and they all cried', and when he rolled out phrases such as 'Ach, it's jist a scunner', laughter and nostalgia combined.

In addition to his North American trips Gordon also visited South Africa where he gave several broadcasts as well as Rhodesia in 1953 going to Bulawayo to take part in the Cecil Rhodes centenary celebrations where he shared the billing with George Formby.

On one North American trip, on board the 'Queen Elizabeth', a special performance was given for passengers by several of the distinguished guests aboard, these included the rather unlikely combination of the Laird of Inversnecky and the French cabaret singer Edith Piaf.

11.   Harry in a 'washing day' pose. No doubt setting the world to rights - or, perhaps, telling tales about the wifie next door.

12.　The famous 'Whistler's Mother' photograph.

13. The Provost of Inversnecky. One of Harry's best loved portrayals.

14.   A fine publicity shot - here captioned with Harry's famous catch phrase
       " 'S Cold Today.".

15.   Harry Gordon in a winter costume for a snow scene. He and Will Fyffe came onto the stage on a sleigh. The date was 1945. Harry commented that although it was a snow scene, the costume 'fair biled' him.

16.   December 1946. Will Fyffe (right) and Harry Gordon open at the Alhambra, Glasgow in 'Babes in the Wood'. This in fact was to be Will Fyffe's last pantomime.

17.　　Mr. and Mrs. Harry Gordon at the Braemar Gathering, 1951.

COMMENCING MONDAY, 16th AUGUST — For a Short Season

NIGHTLY AT 8 p.m.   SATURDAYS ONLY 6 p.m. and 8-30 p.m.

STEWART CRUICKSHANK

presents

Harry Gordon
Jimmy Logan

in Howard & Wyndham's 1954 Edition of

"Half-Past Eight"

A BIGGER and BRIGHTER than ever
SONG, DANCE and LAUGHTER SHOW

with

JACK HOLDEN   HOPE JACKMAN
CLIFF HARLEY

AND FULL COMPANY

Direct from King's Theatre, Edinburgh

Prices :   O.S. 7/-, D.C. 6/-, P.S. 5/-,
C. 4/-, B.S. 3/-, Balcony 2/-.

— BOOK NOW —

18.   Harry - Back at His Majesty's, Aberdeen, August 1954.

19. Harry and Jimmy Logan surrounded by the 'Half Past Eight Girls' at His Majesty's Theatre, Aberdeen. 1954.

20. The Beach Pavilion Aberdeen c. 1959. The scene of so many of Harry's triumphs.

Harry's concert appearances normally comprised over 80 minutes of entertainment, getting through quite a number of songs, character studies and patter divided into three groups. The first consisted of chorus numbers including 'The Call o' the Hielans' which by this time had become his signature tune, 'Doon by the Riverside', 'I belong to Glasgow', 'You can tell a Scot', and 'A Tattie, a Neep and an Ingen'.

The second group consisted of character numbers such as 'The Piper o' Deeside', 'The Auldest Student', 'The Golfer', 'Inversnecky Rangers', 'The Porridge that my Grannie made for me', 'The Story that I startit', and 'The Rodin Tree'.

The final category consisted of Harry's dame studies which included 'The Dowager Duchess', 'The Naafi Cookie', 'The Land Girl' and 'The Brownie'. Harry would select a programme of twelve numbers from these, and although most were well tried and tested, Harry's patter remained topical - one critic referred to the 'up to the minute comedy of Mr Harry Gordon'. Members of the American public used to conjecture 'Why hasn't he got a handle to his name the same as Lauder?' Harry himself was quite happy with compliments such as 'Ye've made up ma mind for me - I'm gaun hame next year.'

9.   FINALE

In the mid 1950's, when the famous 'Half-Past Eight' variety show changed its name to 'Five-Past Eight', Harry Gordon joked to his audiences about the alteration.

"A wifie asked me whit the difference was between 'Half-Past Eight' and 'Five-Past Eight' and I replied "twenty-five minutes". 'Half-Past Eight' and its successor were household names in Glasgow, Edinburgh and Aberdeen for four decades as offering the best in summer variety entertainment.

'Half-Past Eight' was created by Howard and Wyndhams, the theatrical group, who were the propietors of several of the larger Scottish theatres including the King's Theatre, Edinburgh and the Glasgow Theatre Royal in the 1930's. Their intention was to establish a successful summer season show. The comedian in the first 1933 season in Glasgow was Jack Edge who had worked with Harry Gordon in 'The Queen of Hearts' at the King's Theatre, Edinburgh in 1929. Although from Lancashire, Jack Edge was something of a favourite with Scottish audiences and he appeared in variety and pantomime in Scotland until the 1950's.

'Half-Past Eight' did not have a marked initital success but in 1935 Stewart Cruickshank, the managing director, engaged as producer Charles Ross. The first three weeks of this season at the King's Theatre, Edinburgh brought no improvement on previous years; the company played to rows of empty seats. Stewart Cruickshank was in despair, Charles Ross dismayed but determined. Then in the fourth week the 'House Full' boards went up and remained up for 17 weeks. Ross had convinced conservative theatre goers that a song, dance and laughter show with a change of programme every week was something they could not afford to miss. It was a tremendously successful formula which stood up right until the 1960's when television had all but sounded the death knell of the Scottish variety threatre.

Another contributory factor to the sucess of 'Half-Past Eight' was the calibre of the artists, who had to have specialised talent in addition to an extensive repertoire. There were comedians such as George West. West was not a character comedian in the Will Fyffe tradition or a Scotch 'kilt and wiggly walking stick' figure like Sir Harry Lauder, but was one of those handful of Scots comedians like Tommy Lorne, Bert Denver and Jack Anthony, who derived from the English-Italian pantomime clowns. Of the tradition 'on with the motley, the paint and the powder', George West's physical clowning made him a great favourite.

Among other artists who appeared in 'Half-Past Eight' over the years were Billy

Caryll and Hilda Mundy, Syd Seamour and his band, Dick Hurran, Harry Lytton (son of the famous Savoyard, Henry Lytton), Eve Lister and Ann Drummond-Grant. A native of Scotland, Ann Drummond-Grant, tall, handsome and blonde, had been a principal soprano with the D'Oyly Carte Opera Company before the Second World War when she left to do other stage work, including shows in her native country. She eventually returned to Gilbert and Sullivan opera in 1951, her voice considerably deepened and played Gilbert's 'elderly spinster' contralto roles with consummate understanding until her death in 1959. An excellent artist in so many respects she gives further indication of the calibre of supporting artists engaged for 'Half-Past Eight'.

The star of 'Half-Past Eight' in the 1930's was Dave Willis who first appeared in that pioneering 1935 season. Dave had achieved fame when he appeared in the Gaiety Whirls at the Ayr Gaiety from 1931-36. The enterprising Popplewells had provided many young stars with their first success and none greater than Dave Willis. He was unique - his comedy completely spontaneous and original. In direct contrast to Harry Gordon he was never particularly happy when working from a script, but his act included marvellous physical clowning, not of great acrobatic prowess, but in the more delicate mime of the French Jean Gaspard Deburau tradition, and owing something to the influence of Charlie Chaplin. Willis, like so many Scots comedians was content to be local in his humour, but he still appealed to visitors who missed the significance of his Scots phrases by the universal popularity of the 'clown' figure. Dave was well known for his catch phrases including "way, 'way up a 'ky", and when his antics had led him into an embarrassing situaton and the audience were enjoying it - 'it makes you feel such a fool'. The fact that Dave Willis was able to achieve some universality may have had a great deal to do with the fact that his Howard & Wyndham shows established records for their long runs.

Such was the successful background to 'Half-Past Eight' when Harry Gordon joined it in 1943. With the Aberdeen Beach Pavilion now in the past, Harry devoted his summer seasons to 'Half-Past Eight', appearing in Glasgow and Edinburgh while the visits to His Majesty's Theatre in Aberdeen enabled him to maintain contact with his native city. He was devoted to Aberdeen and it meant a tremendous wrench when at the end of the Second World War he decided that as most of his professional commitments were now in Southern Scotland, he would have to sell his house 'Ardeir' at Mannofield, Aberdeen. Nevertheless he soon settled into a luxury flat at Kelvin Court on Great Western Road in Glasgow. On one American tour during a heat-wave in New York, Harry wrote 'I'll be glad to get back to the cool breezes of Anniesland Cross, as well as being his professional base, it was to remain his home for the rest of his life.

Harry retained his tremendous affection for Aberdeen and its neighbourhood. Nevertheless it was with a certain amount of trepidation that he approached his return visits to the city. The size of His Majesty's Theatre meant that he could never achieve the intimate rapport with the audience that was such a remarkable feature of his Beach Pavilion performances. 'Inversnecky' had faded into the background, and Harry Gordon did not use the broad Aberdeen accent as he had done in those old seaside shows. Yet he remained tremendously popular in his native city - and it is true to say that his great regard for Aberdeen was reciprocated by its citizens. On his visits with the 'Half-Past Eight' company, there would be reunions with old friends such as Ada Smith, his former wig mistress and with Percy Forde who played the old Beach Pavilion. Harry would invariably take two or three members of the company on a visit to the Braemar Gathering, while a Saturday afternoon trip to Pittodrie, the home of Aberdeen Football Club, was inevitable. He used to say that it hurt him to tell this gag.

'I hear they're shiftin' the sand aff Aberdeen beach and pittin' it on to Pittodrie'.

'Why, whit for.'

'To keep Aiberdeen frae slippin' into the Second Division'

Among the artists Harry worked with in 'Half-Past Eight' were the faithful Jack Holden, and one of the highlights which remained firmly popular was their front-cloth talk. Inevitably there was one of these just prior to the big production finale and such sketches as 'The Welcome Stranger', 'Slippin' Awa', 'A Helping Hand', continued to delight. Jack Holden who had been associated with Harry Gordon for a great part of his career, and was recognised as one of the most accomplished feeds in the business died in March 1955 in Elgin.

It was a difficult loss to fill but Jack's place was eventually taken by Clement Ashby. Clem had begun his career with the Old Vic and had come North to join Harry Gordon in 'Half-Past Eight' where he became his second feed. Although he worked with Harry for several seasons of 'Half-Past Eight', he curiously never played pantomime with him, and was not an obvious choice of replacement for Jack Holden, as he did not have a broad Scots accent. However, after Harry had auditioned and worked with several comics, he approached Ashby who was then working with Perth Repertory Company, who took on the task of Harry's feed. Clem Ashby was charmed with the invitation, and was delighted at the opportunity of working many of the classic sketches such as the 'Insurance' duo. His style was entirely different to Jack Holden's, but the contrast of character equally effective. Jack Holden, Clem

Ashby and Harry had worked together in such items as 'Whistling Nap' and 'Mother's Coupon'. In the latter item Harry played the wifie checking her football coupon, and getting the names of the teams all wrong. There was Hamilton Accocomicals, Leeds Unitted, Coldham, Aston Vanilla, Smoke City, Ipsiswiches, Heart of Melodeum, and Brum-Brum - Birmingham - 'Who's burning ham'.
The climax occured when having decided she had got them all correct, Mother got up and put on her coat.

"Where are you going?"

"Awa' to post my coupon."

From the audience point of view these sketches were all the more effective because of the seemingly intuitive rapport between the various participants.

Other artists who worked with Harry were Jack Tripp, one time understudy to Sid Field, and later to star in the 'Fol-de-Rols', Cardiff-born Joan Mann, and Stewart and Matthew. Harry had Betty Norton, who was tragically killed in a car crash, as girl feed and then Hope Jackman. She had first been a member of the chorus in the summer show at the King's Theatre in 1937 and ten years later returned as one of the principals, becoming a popular comedienne in her own right as well as a valuable aide to Harry in his comedy sketches. Much has been made of Harry Gordon's verbal brilliance, but one sketch which he did with Hope Jackman was a particular masterpiece of verbal combined with visual skill. In this Harry and Hope played two wifies watching the passers-by. Their eyes would follow an imaginary character walking across the stage in front of them and they would look at her up and down - immediately she disappeared, they would launch into a critical discussion until another imaginary character appeared when a similar process occurred. This required exemplary timing and was extremely effective and funny.

'Half-Past Eight' required a tremendous amount of hard work with its long runs and change of programme every week or fortnight. But Harry Gordon was no stranger to hard work after the summer seasons at the Beach Pavilion and he continued to work as he'd always done into the early hours of the morning drinking milk and writing and revising material.

Harry Gordon is regarded as pioneer of the 'quickie' gag and there were always a few of these just after the opening production number in 'Half-Past Eight.

These are fairly typical:

Harry enters and knocks on an imaginary door (no scenery was ever used - there

71

was no time). A dragon of a woman answers and the following dialogue ensues.

Gordon: Is this the woman's exchange?

Woman: It is.

Gordon: Are you the woman?

Woman: I am.

Gordon: Thanks - I'll just stick to the missus.

     Blackout

There were several 'quickies' in which Harry Gordon and someone else stood at each side of the stage with a torch, which they shone on to their respective faces - this indicated that it was a telephone call. One of these went between Harry and a girl from the telephone exchange.

Gordon: I want to send a telegram to Drumnadrochit

Girl: Drumna - where?

Gordon: Drumnadrochit.

Girl: Can you spell it please?

Gordon: Dear me, lassie, if I could spell it, I'd send a letter.

     Blackout

Jack Holden could play the part of the Presbyterian minister exceptionally well. One gag involved Harry kneeling by a tombstone mouring:

     'Why did you die?; Why did you die? Why did you die?'

Holden walks by and asks:
     'Mouring the loss of a loved one?'

Gordon: 'Not at all - it's my wife's first husband. Why did you die?'
     Why did you die?'

     Blackout

By the late 1940's and early 50's Harry had over two hundred original character studies and more than one hundred duos, which, duly refurbished continued to be popular. But he had to constantly add to his stock of material to maintain topicality. In addition to what he wrote himself, Harry was obliged also to use material contributed by others, but he never found anyone who could produce songs of the calibre of Archie Hyslop's. Nevertheless Joan Benyon, wife of a former manager of the King's Theatre, Edinburgh wrote for him at this time and she produced some successful material including in 1951 a reservist study. Robert Scouler of Paisley also contribuetd sketches such as 'Curly Kwick'.

In spite of all his efforts, however, Harry Gordon found himself from time to time using material of a less sustained high quality than in the 30's and 40's, while he had on occasion to repeat sketches during the run of a show. The majority of the new material did not go down into history and Harry Gordon fell back more and more on the tried and trusted such as 'Mother's Coupon', the 'Insurance' double and 'Rough Hands'. Nevertheless outstanding new items did emerge such as Harry's own big production number 'Strolling down the sunny side of Princes Street'. This was something of a Flanagan and Allen type song, with the performers strolling along as a couple of tramps.

> Strolling along the sunny side of Princes Street
> From the West End to the Waverley
> Fashion on parade, the castle on the rock
> The flowers in full bloom, and, of course the floral clock
> The Boulevards of Paris or Fifth Avenue
> Cannot be compared when you think upon the view you get
> When strolling along the sunny side of Princes Street
> From the West End to the Waverley.

It was against this background that Stewart Cruickshank decided that a second comedian should be engaged to relieve the pressure on Harry, who up to that time had for the most part sustained the comic emphasis on the show itself apart from the occasional routine of Stewart and Matthew. If Harry was not overtly enthusiastic about sharing the place at the top of the bill, he was never openly antagonistic towards those who shared it with him.

In 1952 Harry's co-star was Dickie Henderson. One of the highlights of this show was The Brigton Girls Choir conducted by Miss Petunia Pollock-Shaws. The choirmistress was one of Harry Gordon's perfectly wrought dame studies and such numbers as 'Underneath the Spreading Chestnut Tree' and 'Roll out the Barrel' brought the house down. It was extraordinary how much humour could be extracted from the choir situation particularly as the choirmistress had her back to the audience almost all the time. This was Harry Gordon's middle-aged schoolmistress study - tweed skirt, flat shoes, spectacles on the end of her nose:

Simple ploys such as one of the choir - usually Jack Holden - holding a note after everyone else or dropping the music - the conductor's and the other choir members' reaction giving rise to much mirth - this was a comedy situation with which practically everyone in the audience could identify - one of the bases of good comedy.

In 1953 Reg Varney was the principal guest comedian who was later to make a name for himself in T.V. series such as 'The Rag Trade' and 'On the Buses'.

In the middle 50's two Scottish comedians co-starred with Harry Gordon both of whom subsequently achieved immense success, Jimmy Logan and Stanley Baxter. tanley Baxter is now based in London with extensive professional commitments there. He is still however an extremely versatile first class mimic, sufficiently successful and highly paid that he does not have to run the risk of over exposure. His humour has become cosmopolitan and sophisticated, but in a Glasgow pantomime - and his dame studies are in the classic tradition - he can still have the Glasgow audiences in the palm of his hand.

Jimmy Logan has also achieved a considerable success outside Scotland, but happily he retains much of the traditional Scottish variety theatre. Extremely versatile, one of his successes has been his one-man show 'Lauder'.

Jimmy Logan and Stanley Baxter made a tremendous impact in 'Half-Past Eight' but it was remarkable how well Harry Gordon stood up to these younger Scottish comedians in the 1950's.

Harry Gordon's final appearances in 'Five-Past Eight' were at his favourite Glasgow Alhambra in September 1956, which was starring Jack Radcliffe and Jimmy Logan. Harry returned to the theatre despite his serious heart attack at the end of 1955 and did a short guest spot singing that great old favourite 'The Porridge that my Grannie made for me'.

> Noo grannie's gone, its ages since I heard her accent sharp
> And whiles I wonder how she sounds accompanied on the harp,
> But some day I hope I'll go aloft if only jist tae see
> If they feed her on the porridge that she used tae mak for me'

What an intriguing question!

But the end of an era was at hand. 'Five-Past Eight' continued throughout the sixties, but the impact of T.V. was reducing live variety shows to perilous financial straits. Eventually the Howard and Wyndham theatrical empire was broken up and the great 'Half-Past Eight' and 'Five-Past Eight' shows became just a memory.

10. CURTAIN

On 24th November 1956, Harry Gordon opened at the Theatre Royal, Glasgow with Jack Radcliffe in 'Robinson Crusoe'. This was to be the Theatre Royal's last pantomime before its conversion to S.T.V. television studios. In late December, he was struck down by influenza. His wife kept a constant vigil at his bedside, even when he was transferred to the Royal Infirmary in Glasgow. Harry was held in high regard by his fellow comedians and he had a stream of visitors looking in to cheer him up and bring him the latest theatre news. He was able to joke with his fellow comics but the end was not far off and he died in hospital on Monday, January 21st, 1957 after fighting for 18 days following an operation for thrombosis.

From the age of 15 until he died at 63 Harry Gordon's entire life was devoted to the theatre - a career of 48 years almost without a break. In that time he rose from modest pierrot troupe work to topping the bill in Edinburgh at the King's Theatre, and Theatre Royal, in Glasgow, at the Pavilion, Theatre Royal and Alhambra and at His Majesty's Theatre, Aberdeen. He had taken part in a record breaking series of pantomime successes at the Glasgow Alhambra and was a widely popular and regular radio performer. A biography of Harry Gordon must inevitably to a great extent be the story of his working career. This however in no way understates a loving devotion to his family, particularly his daughter Bunty and his grand-daughter Fiona. Harry Gordon was too busy to pursue many hobbies outside the theatre, although he took up cine-photography enthusiastically and recorded on film scenes from a number of shows, particularly the Glasgow pantomimes. Harry liked to attend the Braemar Gathering whenever possible, and it was a source of pride for him to be presented to King George VI and Queen Elizabeth at the 1951 gathering. He was also a keen Dons fan and regularly attended Aberdeen Football Club's matches. It was not surprising that he returned to the theatre after his serious heart attack in 1955, despite advice to the contrary.

Although he was a great comedian of his era, there was something extraordinarily friendly and unpretentious about Gordon which accounts for his popularity not only with audiences but also amongst members of the profession. Among the latter he was also remembered for his great ability to make every company he worked with a happy and united one. This was what made his concert party at the Beach Pavilion a perennial favourite and contributed to his success in pantomime and in the 'Half-Past Eight' shows. He is also remembered for his absolute insistence on clean wholesome material. In private he might tell a slightly risque joke but these were reserved specifically for all male gatherings. His shows were thus quite consciously 'family' entertainment, a formula which also made sound commercial sense. Similarly he avoided telling jokes which would cast a hurtful slight on any individual person. He was unfailingly kind, charming and helpful to up and coming members of his profession.

In view of the Aberdonian's national reputation, he made the most of the meanness tag. As 'The Auldest Aiberdonian' recalled:

> 'I can min' fin Shakespears acted in a travellin' show
> They chairged ye for admission - so of course I didna' go'

When he was appearing with Jack Radcliffe in Edinburgh, he travelled from Edinburgh to Glasgow every Saturday night in Jack Radcliffe's car. Harry Gordon said he couldn't afford a car but offered to supply a duster for the windscreen - if required. At the end of the twelve week season Harry asked Jack 'What do I owe you for petrol or will you leave it to myself'. Radcliffe replied 'Och, I'll just leave it to you, Harry'. Soon after a registered parcel arrived - a half pound tin of salmon with the note 'from the generous Aberdonian'. However, a short time later a magnificant crystal vase was delivered which became one of the Radcliffe's most treasured possessions. Jack Radcliffe recalling the incident said 'That was the Gordon I knew. A slant of humour in everything he did.'

Earl Wilson, the New York newspaper columnist, recalled Harry Gordon firing a barrage of jokes at him about stingy Scotsmen. 'Why m' laddie', he said, his accent sounding odd in Times Square, 'they say a Scotsman opened his purse and a moth flew out. I claim that's a myth. When I opened my purse last week the moth was dead from lack of fresh air'. Not that in reality he was in the least bit mean, but his charitable work was carried out in a relatively discreet and unobtrusive way. One charity for which he raised money for many years was the East Park Home for Infirm Children in Glasgow.

Harry Gordon was a man of relatively simples tastes - a virtual teetotaller, whose tastes in food included such unpretentious delicacies as cold tripe and potted head. Perhaps his only real extravagances were his holidays in Paris, a city which he loved, while the fashions of that city gave him many useful ideas for dresses and props for his dame studies.

Harry Gordon was a great comedian of his era but the question may be posed - how successful would he have been today in the days of 'permissive' humour delivered without even the subtlety of a Lex McLean! The answer must be that just as he was able to stand up to the younger comedians in the fifties, so in all probability he would have adopted his style and material to suit current trends. The qualities which made him a great performer were universal; his extra-ordinary verbal brilliance, his meticulous attention to every detail of performance and his tireless revision and creation of new material.

Some of Harry Gordon's more popular numbers have been revived by various professional and amateur entertainers. Chief of these is Jimmy Logan who worked with Harry Gordon in pantomime and in 'Half-Past Eight' and greatly admired him. When Logan sings such numbers as 'The story that I startit' he makes no attempt to sing it in the Harry Gordon manner but instead imbues it with a South-west Scotland drawl. In the North East, Robbie Shepherd is a popular local entertainer and his renderings of Harry Gordon songs are always well received while 'Scotland the What' have revived 'The Auldest Aiberdonian' with success. Their style is quite distinctive although there is something of Harry Gordon in their character studies and use of dialect. The road between Inversnecky and Auchterturra is, however, definitely one for the humorist, not the cartographer.

Harry Gordon is remembered throughout Scotland as one of its greatest comedians, and is remembered further afield as a great ambassador. It is in Aberdeen that he is perhaps remembered with greatest affection although it must remain a source for regret that no civic honours were bestowed on him. A commemorative plaque was, however, recently erected on the South Silver Street side of the Music Hall in Aberdeen.

Harry Gordon's body was cremated at Dalgowie Crematorium at Uddingtston, Lanarkshire, on 26th January, 1957. His ashes were then taken North for a memorial service at Gilcomston St. Colm's Church, Aberdeen the following day.

As the people of Aberdeen remembered him, the Rev. Iain Hutcheson spoke for Scots in every clime, but particularly for the folk of Aberdeen and twal' mile roon' when he said: "I believe God used Harry Gordon to bring sunshine into the hearts of many. His was a ministry of laughter, perhaps more effective than the ministry of preaching. 'It's cold today' - so Harry used to say. Well, it's cold today in the hearts of many now that the Laird of Inversnecky has passed on. 'The curtain has come down - but in Harry's ears must ring the tumult of applause. We leave the theatre of his life with happy memories of the Harry we knew - the great comedian, the great actor, the great Scotsman; a great minister of joy and laughter."

APPENDICES

APPENDIX A

BIBLIOGRAPHY

<u>Books</u>

DEVLIN, V.   Kings, Queens and People's Palaces - An Oral History of the
Scottish Variety Theatre. 1920-1970.
Polygon   Edinburgh   1991

HOUSE, J.   Music Hall Memories
Richard Drew Publicity.   Glasgow   1986

IRVING, G.   The Good Auld Days: The Story of Scotland's Entertainers from
Music Hall to Television.
Jupiter Books (London) Ltd. London   1977

LEATHAM, J.   Shows and Showfolk I Have Known: North and South of
the Tweed.
Deveron Press   Turriff   1924

LITTLEJOHN, J. Aberdeen Tivoli
Rainbow Books   Aberdeen   1986

LITTLEJOHN, J. Scottish Music Hall: 1880-1990
G. C. Book Publishers Ltd.   Wigtown   1990

LOCKHART, H. On My Wavelength
Impulse Publications   Aberdeen   1973

MACKIE, A.   The Scottish Comedians
Ramsay Head Press   Edinburgh   1973

MOORE, J.   Ayr Gaiety: The Theatre made famous by the Popplewells
Albyn Press Ltd.   Edinburgh   1976

<u>Newspaper and Magazine Articles</u>

Harry Gordon at the London Palladium. A front page pictorial feature.
    Bon-Accord newspaper, Aberdeen   2/11/29

Harry Gordon - on 'Pantomime'
Bon-Accord Annual   1953   p.38

The Harry Gordon Story
Weekly Scotsman   29/10/59

HUXLEY, J. The Harry Gordon Story. A three part series of articles
Aberdeen Evening Express   20/21/22/6/73

W.D.S.   Archibald Forbes Hyslop - Obituary Notice
Aberdeen Grammar School Magazine   Vol. XLVI No. 2 June 1943

MENZIES, J.   'Hyslopiana'
Aberdeen Grammar School Magazine Vol.LXV No.1 December 1961

TUBERVILLE, R. Harry Gordon's For Me
Scots Magazine   December 1987   p.249

WATSON, I.   A nine part series of articles on Harry Gordon appeared in Leopard
Magazine, Aberdeen between November 1982 and October 1983

A further collection of newscuttings relating to the life and work of Harry Gordon can
be consulted in the Local Studies Department, Aberdeen Central Library.

Programmes 15 Bound Volumes: Harry Gordon's Entertainers - Beach Pavilion
Aberdeen   Covers the years 1924-1938

These volumes can be consulted in the Local Studies Department, Aberdeen Central
Library.

Manuscripts

"Hyslopiana" - Works by Archibald Forbes Hyslop.
Viewing by appointment; Local studies Deparment, Aberdeen Central Library

Song Book

Harry Gordon's Song Hits - Presented by The Sunday Post. 1st September 1935

Further Archival Material relating to Harry Gordon.

Readers should contact:

Elizabeth Watson,
The Scottish Theatre Archive,
Special Collections Dept.,
Glasgow University Library,
Hillhead Street,
GLASGOW.
G12 8QE

DISCOGRAPHY

The discography of Harry Gordon's commercial recordings is compiled from many different sources. Principal amongst these are the record collections of the author himself and those of Duncan Simpson, Gary Anderson, Michael Thomson, Charles Innes and the late Arthur Argo, whose assistance the author gratefully acknowledges. Information generously supplied by the B.B.C. Glasgow has also been incorporated. It is hoped that this listing is complete but if there are any errors or omissions it is certainly not the fault of those good people who provided information.

The records are all 10" 78 r.p.m. with the exception of Beltona 5026 (Fine Man John/ Hilly's Man) which is 12". A number of titles were recorded on both Beltona and Parlophone labels while Beltona re-recorded a few (e.g. The Bells of Inversnecky). Some of the most popular records were pressed several times and in at least one instance - 'A Song of Cove' (Beltona 1370) different 'takes' were used.

EDISON BELL RADIO

1435   Jock's Return on Hogmanay (Parts 1 & 2)
                Jock MacGregor with orch. (really Harry Gordon)

EDISON BELL WINNER

4997   Harry Lauder Melodies (Parts 1 & 2)
                Jock MacGregor with orch. (really Harry Gordon)

5193   Harry Lauder Melodies (Selections 3 & 4)
                Jock MacGregor with orch. (really Harry Gordon)
        (The above two records were re-issued on Mayfair (62097) Harry
        Gordon now becoming Sandy McPhail.)

5290   Pin Your Faith on the Motherland (Milligan/Lauder)
        Doon by the Riverside
                Jock MacGregor with orch. (really Harry Gordon)

5291   The Fleet Pays a Visit (To Auchnatroddie)
                Jock MacGregor with orch. (really Harry Gordon)

ACUTELLE (Pathe Freres Pathephone Ltd.)

10732 If They're Irish (Bring 'Em All In) (Rule-Castling)
    Harry Gordon accomp. piano. by Alice Stephenson

10756 Our Furnished Flat (Squires)
    She Seems to Know (Bennett)
     Harry Gordon piano accomp. Alice Stephenson

BELTONA

1193 The Auldest Aiberdonian (Forbes Hazelwood)
   Dandelions and Daffodils (Damerell-Hargreaves-Bass)
    Harry Gordon/orchestrea

1194 She Dee't (Forbes Hazelwood)
   Fine Man John (Forbes Hazelwood)
    Harry Gordon/orchestra

1295 Himazas
   One and One are Two
    Harry Gordon/orchestra

1296 The Inversnecky Barber (Forbes Hazelwood)
   The Beadle o' Th' Kirk (Forbes Hazelwood)
    Harry Gordon/piano

1297 The Rodin Tree
   Hilly's Man
    Harry Gordon/piano

1368 C.O.N.S.T.A.N.T.I.N.O.P.L.E.
   The Skipper
    Harry Gordon

1369 Fineesh, I go (Geo. Ellis)
   The Ballad Singer (Henry Hedley)
    Harry Gordon

1370   A Song of Cove (Forbes Hazelwood)
               I Wish I was Single Again (Noel Pherns)
               Harry Gordon/orchestra

1427   The Skipper (Clifford Grey)
               One and One are Two
               Harry Gordon/piano/orchestra

1437   A Tattie, A Neep and a Ingin (Forbes Hazelwood)
               The Smith o' Inversnecky (Harry Gordon)
               Harry Gordon/orchestra

1438   The Ghost of Mistress McIntyre (Forbes Hazelwood)
               Better be Lucky Than Beautiful (Wilcock & Rutherford)
               Harry Gordon/orchestra

1439   The Inversnecky Billposter (Forbes Hazelwood)
               The Inversnecky Doctor (Harry Gordon)
               Harry Gordon/orchestra

1440   The Bells of Inversnecky (Forbes Hazelwood)
               The Inversnecky Fireman (Harry Gordon)
               Harry Gordon/orchestra

1473   Inversnecky Moon (Forbes Hazelwood)
               In my Gairden (Harry Gordon)
               Harry Gordon/orchestra

1474   The Story That I Started (Forbes Hazelwood)
               A Limb O' the Law (Harry Gordon)
               Harry Gordon/orchestra

1475   My Inversnecky Lassies (Forbes Hazelwood)
               The Village Editor (Harry Gordon)
               Harry Gordon/orchestra

1476   The Inversnecky Photographer (Forbes Hazelwood)
               The Inversnecky Grocer (H. Toms)
               Harry Gordon/orchestra

1492   The Bells of Inversnecky
        The Inversnecky Billposter
                Harry Gordon. Remade and quite different from titles of
                same name on Nos. 1439 and 1440.

1505   Echoes of Edinburgh (Gordon)
        The Auldest Dame (Gordon)
                Harry Gordon

1506   Grannie's Highland Hame (Sandy MacFarlane)
        Scotland Calling (F. Charles)
                Harry Gordon/orchestra

1507   Turn It Round the Other Way, Timothy (Ed. E. Elton)
        The Kerb Step (C. Knox, D. Street, A. Young)
                Harry Gordon

1508   Caledonia, Hame O' Mine (A. Stroud)
        My Bonnie Jean and I (A. Stanley, A. Klein)
                Harry Gordon

1509   The Fish Shop (Arthur Black)
        The Dentist's Chair (Arthur Black)
                Harry Gordon & Arthur Black

1510   Stung (Arthur Black)
        Parts 1 & 2
                Harry Gordon & Arthur Black

1564   A Mither Aye Kens
        Parts 1 & 2; written by Ruby Slaw
                Bon-Accord Entertainers (i.e. Harry Gordon & A. Black)

1610   The Railway Fireman (Harry Gordon, Jack Holden)
        (The man that maks the smoke come oot the lum) Parts 1 & 2
                Harry Gordon/orchestra

1611   The Piper O' Deeside (Harry Gordon & Jack Holden)
        Parts 1 & 2
        Harry Gordon/orchestra

1625 The Inversnecky Bus (Harry Gordon)
  The Lassie That I Love so Well (Strone-Johnston)
   Harry Gordon/orchestra

1638 Where Is My Wandering Boy (Forbes Hazelwood)
  Parts 1 & 2
   Harry Gordon/orchestra

1652 Passing The Time
  Parts 1 & 2
   Harry Gordon & Donald Hunter

1653 The Inversnecky Anthem (Forbes Hazelwood)
  The Society Man (Harry Gordon)
   Harry Gordon/orchestra

1678 Bleak House
  Parts 1 & 2
   Harry Gordon & Jack Holden

1679 My Dear Wee Cat (Ruby Slaw)
  Shavin' Masel' (Stone Johnstone)
   Harry Gordon

1693 The Call O' Th' Hielans (Harry Gordon)
  Parts 1 & 2
   Harry Gordon/orchestra

1697 His First Nicht Out (Gordon & Hunter)
  Parts 1 & 2
   Harry Gordon & Donald Hunter

1723 Sing Me A Hebridean Song (Forbes Hazelwood)
  The Village Dominie (Corrie and Gordon
   Harry Gordon/orchestra

1724 At the Grocers (Harry Gordon & Donald Hunter)
  Parts 1 & 2
   Harry Gordon & Donald Hunter

1754	Aberdeen v. Queen's park
	(1) On the Way (2) At the Match
	Harry Gordon & Jack Holden

1755	The Champion Boxer (Harry Gordon & Jack Holden)
	The Scaffie (Harry Gordon & Jack Holden)
	Harry Gordon/orchestra

1765	The Parliamentary Candidate (Harry Gordon & Jack Holden)
	Parts 1 & 2
	Harry Gordon & Jack Holden

1768	I Love The Spring (Harry Gordon & S. Glen)
	When the Broom Blooms Bricht on the Bonnie Broomielaw (Garth Navy)
	Harry Gordon/orchestra

1779	Hiking
	Parts 1 & 2
	Harry Gordon & Jack Holden

1782	Drambuie Blues (Harry Gordon)
	The Lassie That I'm Coortin Noo (Gordon & Glen)
	Harry Gordon/orchestra

1799	The Convict's Lament (Gordon)
	The Ploughboy (Gordon)
	Harry Gordon

1800	Grousin on The Moors
	Parts 1 & 2
	Harry Gordon & Jack Holden

1815	The Explorer (Jack Holden & Harry Gordon)
	The Auldest Student (Flanagan, Gordon)
	Harry Gordon/orchestra

1823	Scotland Is Calling To Me (John P. Ross)
	It's Fine to Hae A Placie O' Yer Ain (Wilkie Graham)
	Harry Gordon

1824	The Stage Cleaners
	Parts 1 & 2
	Harry Gordon & Jack Holden

1824   The Stage Cleaners
Parts 1 & 2
    Harry Gordon & Jack Holden

1841   The Washing Day
Parts 1 & 2
    Harry Gordon & Jack Holden

1842   The Inversnecky Lifeboat
The Inversnecky Waiter
    Harry Gordon

1859   The Porter and The Pro
Parts 1 & 2
    Harry Gordon & Jack Holden

1860   The Lighthouse Keeper
Our New House
    Harry Gordon/orchestra

1861   Put Them Amang The Lassies
What's The Use
    Harry Gordon

1882   On The Saucy Arethusa
Parts 1 & 2
    Harry Gordon & Jack Holden

1891   My Auld Tin Hat (Holden, Gordon)
Inversnecky Cobbler (Holden, Gordon)
    Harry Gordon/orchestra

1903   At the BBC
Parts 1 & 2
    Harry Gordon & Jack Holden

1904   Stovies (Forbes Hazelwood)
The Inversnecky Golfer (Forbes Hazelwood)
    Harry Gordon/orchestra

1905	Mrs. McIntyre Visits the Sick
	Parts 1 & 2
	Harry Gordon & Arthur Black
1915	Princes Street (Hazelwood, Hyslop)
	Mairret (Gordon)
	Harry Gordon
1921	My Affinity (H. Gordon)
	Lady Of My Dreams (H. Gordon)
	The Pavilion Guisers Vocal Chorus/Harry Gordon
1923	My Pal Wullie
	Inversnecky Postie
	Harry Gordon
1925	Seeing The Toon
	Parts 1 & 2
	Harry Gordon & Jack Holden
1928	At the Photographers
	Parts 1 & 2
	Harry Gordon & Arthur Black
1936	The Charwoman
	Parts 1 & 2
	Harry Gordon & Arthur Black
1937	The Inversnecky Stores
	Parts 1 & 2
	Harry Gordon & Jack Holden
1938	A Permanent Wave
	Parts 1 & 2
	Harry Gordon & Jack Holden
1939	Eppie The Auld Fish Wife
	The Porridge That My Grannie Made For Me
	Harry Gordon/orchestra

1955	On A Pillion
	Parts 1 & 2
	Harry Gordon & Jack Holden

1956	The Pedlar
	The Village Baker
	Harry Gordon

2004	Late Night Final
	Parts 1 & 2
	Harry Gordon & Jack Holden

2075	Advertising
	Parts 1 & 2
	Harry Gordon & Jack Holden

2150	Brutus The Roman Scot (J. Holden & H. Gordon)
	The Village Bellman (D. Bruce & H. Gordon)
	Harry Gordon accomp. by Alice Stephenson

2204	The Pool at Aiberdeen
	In the Simmertime
	Harry Gordon accomp. by Alice Stephenson

BL 2503	The Land Girl (Harry Gordon)
	The Call O' The Hielans (Harry Gordon)
	Harry Gordon with Roy Robertson & his orchestra

BL 2504	The Lass I'm Courtin' Noo (Harry Gordon)
	The Dowager Duchess (Harry Gordon)
	Harry Gordon with Roy Robertson & his orchestra

5026	Fine Man John (Forbes Hazelwood)
	Hilly's Man (Harry Gordon)
	Harry Gordon/orchestra

PARLOPHONE

R479   The Inversnecky Fireman
Fine Man John
        Harry Gordon

R480   Inversnecky Blues (Forbes Hazelwood)
Bells of Inversnecky (Forbes Hazelwood)
        Harry Gordon

R513   The Inversnecky Photographer (Forbes Hazelwood)
The Village Editor (Harry Gordon
        Harry Gordon/piano

R514   In My Gairden (Harry Gordon)
The Limb O' The Law (Harry Gordon)
        Harry Gordon/piano

R515   The Inversnecky Doctor
The Village Grocer (Toms & Gordon)
        Harry Gordon

R516   Inversnecky Moon (Forbes Hazelwood)
Story That I Started (Forbes Hazelwood)
        Harry Gordon

R603   The Weddin' O' Wee MacGregor (Fred Godfrey & Harry Gordon)
Flittin (R. Rutherford - Frank Wilcock)
        Harry Gordon/orchestra

R633   Golf (Harry Gordon & Jack Holden)
Parts 1 & 2
        Harry Gordon & Jack Holden/piano

R635   Joining The Force (Gordon & Holden)
Parts 1 & 2
        Harry Gordon & Jack Holden

R634	The Compleat Anglers (Harry Gordon & Jack Holden) Parts 1 & 2 Harry Gordon & Jack Holden/piano
R636	The Piano Tuners Parts 1 & 2 Harry Gordon & Jack Holden
R811	The Auldest Aiberdonian (Forbes Hazelwood) Hilly's Man (Harry Gordon) Harry Gordon/orchestra
R829	The Auld Scotch Mither O' Mine (Forbes Hazelwood) The Sea Cook (Gordon & Holden) Harry Gordon/orchestra
R830	The Labour Exchange Parts 1 & 2 Harry Gordon & Jack Holden
R869	Snecky Station Gig (Gordon & Holden) Inversnecky Rangers (Gordon & Holden) Harry Gordon
R1029	The Clerk O' The Weather The Commercial Traveller Harry Gordon
R1030	His Weddin Morn Parts 1 & 2 Harry Gordon & Jack Holden
R1103	Discord Parts 1 & 2 Harry Gordon & Jack Holden
R1649	The Welcome Stranger Parts 1 & 2 Harry Gordon & Jack Holden/piano

R1650	Slippin' Awa' Parts 1 & 2 Harry Gordon & Jack Holden
R1651	Questionnaire Parts 1 & 2 Harry Gordon & Jack Holden
R1652	Dyspeptic (F. Hazelwood) Sandy MacSporran (Harry Gordon) Harry Gordon
R1653	Mindin' The Cars in the Park Pancake That My Sweetie Made For Me Harry Gordon
F3007	Fine Man John Inversnecky Fireman Harry Gordon
F3008	Bells of Inversnecky Inversnecky Blues Harry Gordon
F3001	Village Grocer Inversnecky Doctor Harry Gordon
F3014	Hilly's Man Auldest Aiberdonian Harry Gordon
F3017	Clerk of The Weather Commercial Traveller Harry Gordon
F3018	Dyspeptic Sandy MacSporran Harry Gordon

F3019   Pancake That My Sweetie Made
              Mindin' The Cars
                   Harry Gordon

F3020   Inversnecky Medley
              Parts 1 & 2
                   Harry Gordon

F3021   Golf
              Parts 1 & 2
                   Harry Gordon & Jack Holden

APPENDIX C

HARRY GORDON IN PANTOMIME

Up to 1929 Harry Gordon was a member of various touring pantomime companies which performed in many of the smaller Scottish theatres.

1929   Queen of Hearts - King's Theatre, Edinburgh
A Julian Wylie production in which Harry Gordon starred with the Lancashire comedian, Jack Edge.

1930   Mother Goose - King's Theatre, Edinburgh
The hit song of the pantomime was 'Where is My Wandering Boy To-day'.

1931   Dick Whittington - Theatre Royal Glasgow
The dame part was played by Tom D. Newell, the hit song 'When the Broom Blooms Bricht on the Bonnie Broomielaw'.

1932   Jack and the Beanstalk - King's Theatre, Edinburgh.

1933   Red Riding Hood - Theatre Royal, Edinburgh

1934   Rip Van Winkle - Theatre Royal, Edinburgh

1935   Humpty Dumpty - Theatre Royal, Edinburgh

1936   Babes in the Wood - Theatre Royal, Edinburgh

1933-1936 Pantomimes moved on from Edinburgh for seasons at the Glasgow Pavilion.

1937   Puss in Boots - Glasgow Alhambra - the first of the great Alhambra series.

1938   Aladdin - Glasgow Alhambra
Widow Twankey was Harry Gordon's first dame part since 1930.

1939   Cinderella - Glasgow Alhambra

1940   The Sleeping Beauty - Glasgow Alhambra

1941   Dick Whittington - Glasgow Alhambra
This was Harry Gordon's first pantomime co-starring with Will Fyffe.

1942   Jack and The Beanstalk - Glasgow Alhambra
The hit song was Harry Gordon's 'The Land Girl'.

1943   Red Riding Hood - Glasgow Alhambra
The hit song was Harry Gordon's 'The Happy Naafi Cook'

1944   Robinson Crusoe - Glasgow Alhambra
This produced was one of Harry Gordon's most popular numbers 'One of the oldest hens in the W.R.N.S.'

1945   King and Queen of Hearts - Glasgow Alhambra
One of Harry Gordon's most popular numbers was 'Katie the Queen of the Clippies'.

1946   Babes in the Wood - Glasgow Alhambra
This was Will Fyffe's last pantomime.

1947   Humpty Dumpty - Glasgow Alhambra
Alec Finlay took Will Fyffe's place.

1948   Puss in Boots - Glasgow Alhambra
Harry Gordon had two popular numbers 'Tessie the Toast of the Trossachs;' and 'Steamie Jeanie'.

1949   Dick Whittingon - Glasgow Alhambra

1950   Cinderella - Glasgow Alhambra
The stars of the pantomime were Harry Gordon, Alec Finlay, Robert Wilson and Duncan Macrae.

1951   Aladdin - Glasgow Alhambra

1952   Jack and The Beanstalk - Glasgow Alhambra
The last of the Alhambra series.

1953   Puss in Boots - Theatre Royal, Glasgow
Harry Gordon starred with Jimmy Logan.

1954   Dick Whittington - King's Theatre, Edinburgh
Harry Gordon starred with Jack Radcliffe

1955   Dick Whittington - Theatre Royal, Glasgow
Harry Gordon missed this pantomime because of illness. His
place was taken by Andy Stewart.

1956   Robinson Crusoe - Theatre Royal, Glasgow
Harry Gordon's last pantomime during the run of which he fell
ill and died - his part was taken over by Aly Wilson.

ARCHIVE MATERIAL HELD BY **THE SCOTTISH FILM ARCHIVE**, 74 Victoria Crescent Road, Dowanhill, Glasgow. G12 9JN Tel. 041-334 4445 Fax. 041-334 8132

Please note that titles marked REF denote preservation material for which no viewing copies exist.

Titles marked VIEW indicate that a viewing copy is available.

MUSIC HALL AND PANTOMIME

1133   [HALF PAST EIGHT SHOW]

b/w silent   REF
Copyright   Mrs. Bunty MacLeod

Filmed during the dress rehearsal of the "Half Past Eight" show starring Harry Gordon, Betty Jumel, Margaret Holden, Georgina Jumel and Bunty Gordon.

335 ft   amateur

1134   [ROBINSON CRUSOE 1944]

b/w and col. silent   1944   REF
Copyright   Mrs. Bunty MacLeod

Footage of a summer show, probably in Aberdeen's Beach Pavilion, starring Harry Gordon with shots of an acrobatic act, highland dancing and Harry Gordon starting off a tug-of-war contest.

423 ft   amateur

1135   [CINDERELLA 1950   ALADDIN 1951]

col. silent   1950/51   REF
Copyright   Mrs. Bunty MacLeod

Scenes from pantomimes "Cinderella" and "Aladdin". Harry Gordon and Duncan Macrae are the Ugly sisters.

387 ft.   amateur

1136   [CINDERS 1950 and ROAD SHOW, DUNDEE]

b/w and col. silent   REF
Copyright   Mrs. Bunty MacLeod

Shots of a pantomime from the wings and balcony of a theatre, probably the Alhambra in
Glasgow. The film also includes footage of a roadshow in Dundee, starring Harry Gordon.

369 ft .   amateur

1137   [ROBINSON CRUSOE 1944]

col. silent   1944/45   REF
Copyright   Mrs. Bunty MacLeod

Scenes from the pantomime "Robinson Crusoe" starring Harry Gordon and Will Fyffe.

400 ft.   amateur

1138   [ALADDIN 1938]

b/w silent   1938   REF
Copyright   Mrs. Bunty MacLeod

Scenes from the pantomime "Aladdin" at the Glasgow Alhambra. Cast includes Harry
Gordon, Alex Finlay and Jack Holden.

416 ft.   amateur

1139   [KING AND QUEEN OF HEARTS 1945]

col. silent   1945   VIEW
Copyright   Mrs. Bunty MacLeod

Footage of the pantomime "King and Queen of Hearts", cast includes Harry Gordon
and Will Fyffe.

399 ft.   amateur

1140   [VARIOUS ARTISTS]

b/w and col. silent   REF
Copyright   Mrs. Bunty MacLeod

Scenes from various pantomimes and variety shows featuring Harry Gordon, Alec
Finlay, Dave Willis, Florrie Forde, and Alec Lennox.

480 ft.   amateur

1141   [KING AND QUEEN OF HEARTS 1945]

b/w silent   VIEW
Copyright   Mrs. Bunty MacLeod

Scenes from the stage pantomime "King and Queen of Hearts" and various sketches
featuring Harry Gordon, Jack Anthony, Will Fyffe and Jack Holden.

402 ft.   amateur

1142   [RED RIDING HOOD 1943]

b/w and col. silent   1943   VIEW
Copyright   Mrs. Bunty MacLeod

Scenes from the stage pantomime "Red Riding Hood" including shots of Harry Gordon
in his dressing room and Will Fyffe in costume.

345 ft.   amateur

1143   [PANTOMIME AND CHRISTMAS PARTY]

b/w and col. silent   1943   REF
Copyright   Mrs. Bunty MacLeod

Shots of pantomime troupe performing with Harry Gordon and their Christmas party
in the Adelphi Hotel, Glasgow.

210 ft.   amateur

1144   [HALF PAST EIGHT SHOW 1945 AND ROBINSON CRUSOE PARTY 1944]

col. silent   REF
Copyright   Mrs. Bunty MacLeod

Song and dance routines and comedy sketches from the "Half Past Eight Show" and "Robinson Crusoe" featuring Harry Gordon and Will Fyffe.

401 ft.   amateur

1145   [THE SLEEPING BEAUTY 1940]

b/w and col. silent   REF
Copyright   Mrs. Bunty MacLeod

Shots of pantomime "The Sleeping Beauty" featuring Harry Gordon as the "Queen" and Alec Finlay as the "King".

420 ft.   amateur

1146   [BABES IN THE WOOD 1936]

col. silent   1936   REF
Copyright   Mrs. Bunty MacLeod

Filmed during the dress rehearsal of the pantomime "Babes in the Wood" featuring Harry Gordon in various sketches.

267 ft.   amateur

1147   [HUMPTY DUMPTY 1947]

b/w and col. silent   1947   REF
Copyright   Mrs. Bunty MacLeod

General views of the dress rehearsal of the pantomime "Humpty Dumpty", starring Harry Gordon, Duncan Macrae and Alec Finlay.

380 ft.   amateur

1149   [DICK WHITTINGTON 1941]

col. silent   REF
Copyright   Mrs. Bunty MacLeod

Filmed during the dress rehearsal of the pantomime "Dick Whittington" featuring
Harry Gordon and Will Fyffe - Glasgow Alhambra.

300 ft.   amateur

1150   [PANTOMIME, SHOW PICNIC AND VARIETY]

b/w and col. silent   1939/42   VIEW
Copyright   Mrs. Bunty MacLeod

Shots of Harry Gordon and Will Fyffe in the pantomime "Jack and the Beanstalk" -
1942. The film also shows a picnic for members of the cast.

399 ft.   amateur

1151   [BEACH PAVILION, ABERDEEN AND FAMILY c. 1926]

b/w silent   REF
Copyright   Mrs. Bunty MacLeod

Harry Gordon and company star in a variety show at the Beach Pavilion, Aberdeen.

246 ft.   amateur

1152   [BEACH PAVILION, ABERDEEN AND VARIETY]

b/w and col. silent
Copyright   Mrs. Bunty MacLeod

Scenes at a variety show in the Beach Pavilion, Aberdeen; Harry Gordon in "Puss in
Boots" and a varity show in the Alhambra Theatre, Glasgow. [Note: There were 2
"Puss in Boots" at the Alhambra, 1937 and 1938. Since the film also features the Beach
Pavilion, this is possibly the earlier].

440 ft.   amateur

INDEX